PASTA VERDE

PASTA VERDE

Judith Barrett

MACMILLAN · USA

MACMILLAN
A Simon & Schuster Macmillan Company
1633 Broadway
New York, NY 10019

Paperback Edition 1998

MACMILLAN is a registered trademark of Macmillan, Inc.

Library of Congress Cataloging-in-Publication Data
Barrett, Judith
Pasta verde/Judith Barrett
p. cm.
Includes index.
ISBN: 978-0-02-862286-6
1. Cookery (Pasta) 2. Vegetarian cookery. I. Title.
TX 809. M17B36 1995
641. 8'22—dc20   94-47297
CIP

Macmillan Publishing books may be purchased for business or sales promotional use.
For information please write: Special Markets Department, Macmillan Publishing USA,
1633 Broadway, New York, NY 10019.

Design by Janet Tingey

DEDICATION

For my parents,
George and Mitzi Silver

▦ ACKNOWLEDGMENTS

I want to thank the many people who assisted me in my research for this book. Elizabeth Kane and The Italian Trade Commission were extremely helpful in making contacts for me in Italy. Corby Kummer, Lynn Kasper, Carol Field, Anna Teresa Callen, and Nancy Radke were all generous with their tips and leads.

In Italy I am grateful to Dr. Rocco Bagnato and Alberto Ventura in the Department of Agriculture of Regione Emilia Romagna; Marco Bonati at Barilla Alimentare SpA in Parma; Lagorio Rag. Lorenzo of Raineri SpA in Imperia; Mario Zannoni of the Consorzio Parmigiano Reggiano in Parma; and Franco Colombani at the Albergo del Sole in Maleo for inviting me into his kitchen.

Daphne Rota gave me great assistance in testing recipes. Ishan Gurdal was invaluable in fulfilling my requests for cheeses.

I am indebted to my agent, Bob Cornfield, for his efforts on my behalf, and my editor, Pam Hoenig, for her continuing support of my work.

I want to especially thank my sister, Jane, for traveling with me to Italy; my children, Annie and Rachel; and all my family and friends who are great supporters and loving critics. I am most thankful to my husband, David, whose love of eating is perfectly matched to mine of cooking.

❖ CONTENTS

❖ INTRODUCTION

Cucina verde is what vegetarian cooking is called in Italy. Its closest literal translation, *green cuisine*, calls to mind our varied efforts to live in closer harmony with the natural world, from cooking with fresh and unprocessed ingredients to softening our impact on the world itself.

This book is a celebration of the versatility, convenience, and capacity for innovation of pasta and vegetables. It is my invitation to you to bring home whatever green (or red, yellow, orange, or white) vegetables are fresh and available in your market—be it a farmstand, greengrocer, or mega-supermarket—and my assurance that you will find in *Pasta Verde* a wide choice of recipes for quickly preparing healthy and delicious pasta sauces, soups and salads, and heart-healthy low-fat recipes.

In writing this book I have had the pleasure of searching for inspiration in Italy and refining the recipes and techniques by cooking for my family and friends. All of the recipes are simple to prepare, use Italian cooking methods and ingredients, and are part of a healthy diet. I hope you find the results to be delicious and inviting dishes that will secure a place for *Pasta Verde* at your table.

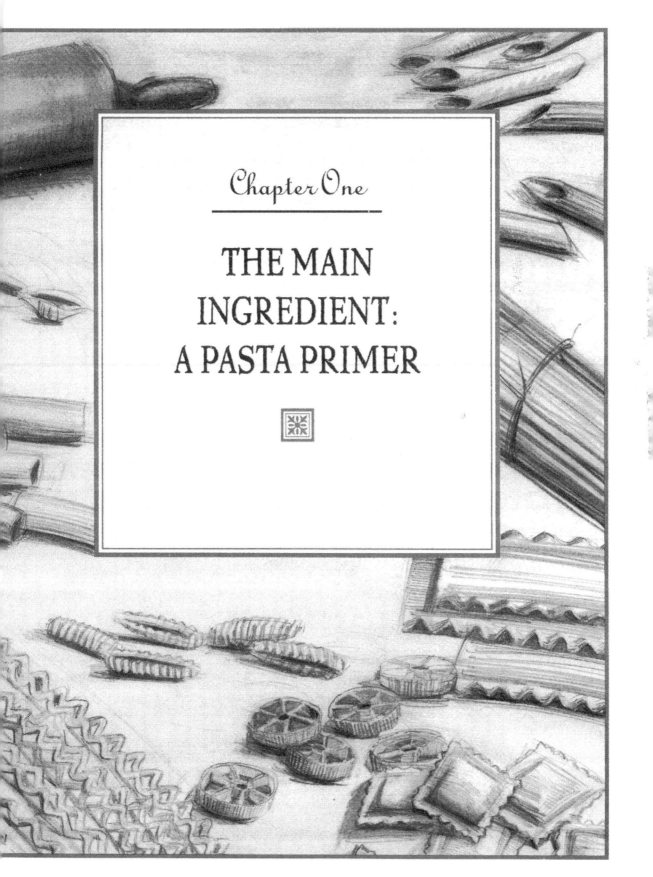

Chapter One

THE MAIN INGREDIENT: A PASTA PRIMER

PASTA'S PAST

As much as we may like the familiar story of Marco Polo bringing spaghetti to Italy from Asia, most food historians now agree that the roots of pasta in Italy are to be found in the Middle East rather than the Far East.

Earliest records show that the ancient Romans prepared a type of pasta they called, in Latin, *laganum*, a cake made with strips of dough that was adopted from the Greeks and is now considered to be the forerunner of *lasagna*. But pasta as we know and love it—strands of noodles served shimmering with sauce—entered the Italian culinary tradition centuries later with the invasion of Sicily by Moslem Arabs after 800 A.D. The Moslems were known to have noodles in their native domains and presumably brought them along on their conquests. The first recorded mention of pasta in Italy was in 1150 A.D. when it was noted in a Sicilian geographer's survey of farmland as *itriya*, an Arabic word for pasta. He wrote that the land was suitable for growing the wheat used for making the pasta. Later called *vermicelli di tria*, pasta is still called *tria* in Sicilian dialect. Elsewhere in Italy, pasta—which is also the generic name for any dough or paste in Italian (*pasta frolla* is puff pastry, and *pasta di mandorla* is marzipan or almond paste)—has become the single word for all types and shapes of noodles.

In pasta's early days it was prepared by cooks at home. In the seventeenth century, pasta began to be prepared and sold commercially like bread in individual shops. However, the methods of production at the time produced a pasta that did not keep well, and its perishability made it less appealing. That changed in 1800 when it was discovered that air-drying the dough alternately in hot and cool temperatures would eliminate the moisture without leaving the dough brittle. With that advancement, pasta's popularity took off. The town of Torre Annunziata near Naples was found to have the perfect conditions for this drying process, and that is where the industry of pasta manufacturing began and continues today.

Gradually, all dry pasta production was moved from small shops to large factories where the process—combining the hard durum wheat flour and water to make the dough, rolling and cutting the dough, and finally drying the pasta shapes—was expanded and completely mechanized. With expansion and mechanization, pasta finally became an integral part of Italian life, and the culinary cornerstone of the Italian meal.

DRY PASTA

Of the two basic types of pasta eaten in Italy—fresh and dry—the most prevalent and popular is plain, dry pasta. Called *pasta secca*, which means *dry pasta*, and sometimes *pasta asciutta*, which means *drained pasta*, to distinguish it from pasta served in broth or soup, dry pasta is a manufactured product, produced in factories and sold in bags or boxes or in bulk in markets. But all dry pasta is not created equal. What most distinguishes Italian-made pastas from their American counterparts is the type of wheat used to make the flour to manufacture the pasta. Most Italian *pasta secca* is made only with flour from hard durum wheat. That flour gives the pasta its defining characteristics: a firm, chewy texture and an almost nutty flavor when cooked.

In contrast, most American-made dry pasta, which emerged with the waves of immigration at the turn of the twentieth century, is manufactured with a blend of hard and soft wheat flours. All companies don't use the same blend, but the addition of flour from soft wheat gives the cooked pasta noticeably less flavor and a more supple texture after it is cooked.

An important difference among Italian dry pastas is the type of manufacturing process the producer uses. Some smaller, older pasta factories in Italy still use machines with brass dies (newer machines have teflon-coated dies) to press out the pasta shapes, and workers who air dry and pack every piece of pasta by hand. These pastas—Martelli from Tuscany and Rustichella from Abruzzo to name two—are sold in specialty food stores for three to four times what most imported dry pasta costs. Because the pieces of pasta are extruded through brass dies, they have a coarser texture on the outer surface of the individual pieces of pasta than pasta from teflon-coated dies. The rougher outer surface enhances the pasta in two ways: it gives the cooked pasta a more chewy texture and helps to hold the sauce on the pasta. The difference is subtle, but some pasta lovers find it worth the extra cost.

Most Italian pasta, however, is manufactured in big modern plants with machinery that automatically extrudes, cuts, dries, and packs their product. Barilla is the largest manufacturer of pasta in Italy, and I visited the Barilla factory near Parma, 1 of 30 they have throughout Italy. These factories each produce up to 2 million pounds of pasta a day and 100 different shapes. That's enough pasta for 10 million meals. The factory was impressive for its size — as big as several airplane hangars — as well as for its automation. The people who showed me around were very proud of how few workers are needed to run the enormous machines which, with the help of computers, do everything from mill the flour and form and dry the pasta, to stick packing labels on the filled, finished boxes.

Yet another, significant difference in pastas is that all pasta sold in the United States — whether it's made here or in Italy — must meet FDA standards by being enriched with vitamins. (You may notice that all pasta packaging states clearly that it is an "enriched macaroni product.") As a result, Italian pasta manufacturers use different ingredients in the pasta production for export to this country and frequently have separate sections of their factories devoted to this production. This means that Italian pasta bought in the United States is not the same as pasta bought in Italy no matter how old or new the factory. However, because the type of wheat used to make the pasta has the greatest effect on taste and texture, most people in the industry say that the enrichment has little, if any, effect on the quality of the finished product.

My own taste buds tell me that I prefer the taste and texture of Italian brands made with only hard durum wheat flour and water over American brands. And fortunately, many Italian brands are available in supermarkets here and cost little more than their American counterparts, although the specific brands available may vary from region to region across the United States. Of the imported Italian products, Barilla, DeCecco, and Delverde are my favorite brands. I always keep a variety of shapes in my cupboard.

The most popular and available shapes—and the shapes called for in most of the recipes in this book—include the following:

penne/pennette	quills/little quills
mostaccioli	
farfalle	bow ties
rigatoni	fat tubes
ziti	thin tubes
fusilli/rotini	squiggles
cavatappi	corkscrews
conchiglie	shells
tubetti/ditallini	small tubes
rotelli	wheels
orecchiette	little ears/disks
orzo	barley shape
spaghetti/spaghettini	thin strands/thinner strands
linguine	flat, narrow strands
fettucine	flat, wide strands
pappardelle	wide strips
lasagne	very wide strips

FRESH PASTA

Generally made with all-purpose white flour and whole eggs, fresh pasta is most characteristic of Northern Italian cooking, although it can be found in restaurants and homes throughout Italy. The best fresh pasta is the kind you make yourself from scratch, and for those who have the inclination, homemade pasta has deliciously memorable rewards: Each bite is extraordinarily tender, delicate, and light, and almost melts in your mouth. What's more, you can cut it any way you want—in sheets for *lasagna*, wide strands for *pappardelle*, or squares for *ravioli*, all of which are not widely available commercially.

Preparing fresh pasta is surprisingly easy and satisfying, but it is also time-consuming and messy. Even so, I wholeheartedly recommend it. You can either mix the dough by hand, which allows you to gauge by feel just how much flour should be added to the eggs, or make the pasta dough in a food processor. Recipes for both are included in this chapter.

Fresh pasta made in Italian homes is sometimes made all by hand, from mixing, to rolling, to cutting the dough. More often it is made with the help of a pasta machine. Two types of pasta machines are available: hand-cranked and electric. Electric models do everything from mixing the dough from raw ingredients to extruding out strands and a variety of shapes. These electric models are easy to use, but the pasta dough they turn out isn't as thin or as tender as it should be.

For melt-in-your-mouth quality pasta, by far the best choice in pasta machines is the most economical and least expensive—the hand-cranked model. Made in Italy and preferred by Italian cooks, these hand-powered machines help you to knead the dough and roll it out into strips which are the perfect length for lasagna, or cut it into strands for fettucine or spaghetti.

I have used a hand-cranked pasta machine for many years and recommend it to anyone interested in making fresh pasta. The Atlas pasta machine is probably the most widely available (it is also available with a motor attachment). It stands about 6 inches high and 10 inches wide; attaches temporarily or permanently with a built-in screw and clamp to any kitchen counter; and is light and compact enough to store in a cupboard. After you make the dough (see page 8), the pasta machine helps to knead and roll it. It has one side for rolling the dough between two rollers that can be adjusted for thickness, and one side for cutting rolled strips into strands. I've had my machine for about 15 years, and I still keep it in the box it came in to prevent it from getting dusty when I'm not using it. I never wash it—small pieces of dough or flour left in the machine will get wet and can clog the rolling mechanism—but I do shake it out and wipe it down with a damp sponge after each use. It may not be absolutely essential for rolling out pasta dough—you can use good old elbow grease and a rolling pin—but it makes the job much easier.

When you make fresh pasta, you need some way to dry it if you don't intend to cook it right away. A framed screen is the preferred tool for drying flat pasta shapes, including ravioli and other filled pasta. A solid flat surface like a cookie sheet is not recommended for drying filled pasta; the pasta turns soggy and sticks to the surface. Something you can hang pasta on is essential for drying the long strands. Both types of drying racks are available in good kitchenware stores.

▧ HANDMADE FRESH PASTA DOUGH

Fresh pasta dough is a combination of eggs and flour. For best results, I recommend using unbleached, all-purpose flour. You can also use whole wheat flour, durum wheat flour, or grainy semolina; but each yields a different result. This basic recipe makes one pound of dough. It can be increased or decreased according to your needs. Variations for using your food processor and preparing flavored pastas follow.

1 POUND OF DOUGH, APPROXIMATELY 4 SERVINGS

About 2 1/2 cups all-purpose flour
3 extra-large eggs
1/4 teaspoon kosher salt

To mix the dough. Pile the flour onto a clean work surface. Make a well in the center and break the eggs into it; add the salt to the eggs. Using a fork, beat the eggs while gradually incorporating the flour into them. When you can form a ball of dough, knead it with your hands on the floured work surface, incorporating more flour as needed until the dough is soft and malleable. If you intend to roll the dough with a rolling pin, knead the dough for approximately 10 minutes. If you intend to roll the dough through a pasta machine, knead the dough for 5 minutes. Cover the dough with plastic wrap and allow it to rest unrefrigerated about 15 minutes before you roll it out or run it through a pasta machine.

To roll the dough with a rolling pin. Place the ball of dough on a lightly floured work surface and flatten it down with the heel of your hand. Use a lightly floured rolling pin to roll it out to the desired degree of thinness. Pasta is usually rolled out to about $1/32$-inch thick. As you roll, keep the work surface, rolling pin, and dough lightly floured so that the dough doesn't stick. When the dough is completely rolled out, cut it into the desired shape.

To roll the dough by machine. Divide the dough into two or three pieces. Flatten each piece of dough with your hand so that it is approximately $1/2$-inch thick. Turn the gauge on the pasta machine's smooth roller to its widest (lowest) setting. Lightly flour the dough before feeding it through the rollers. After the dough comes through the machine, fold it into thirds, lightly flour it again, and press it down with your fingers to remove as much air as possible. Run the dough through the machine again on the widest setting, feeding the open end in first. Repeat this 3 or 4 times until the dough is smooth. Reduce the setting on the gauge one notch. Lightly flour the dough and, without folding it, run it through the rollers. Continue to narrow the width of the rollers one notch after each pass through of the dough until you reach the highest (narrowest) setting. Because pasta machines differ, you may not be able to roll out the pasta on the highest (narrowest) setting without breaking the dough. As the strip of dough becomes very long, cut it in half to make it easier to handle. Lightly flour the strip of dough before passing it through the machine each time.

To cut the dough. When the dough has been rolled as thinly as possible, by hand or by machine, you can cut it to the desired shape. Most pasta machines offer at least two cutting dies with a wider and narrower width. I usually prefer to cut the pasta by hand. When cutting wider shapes—pappardelle, ravioli, lasagna—I simply place the long strips of dough on a cutting board dusted with flour or semolina and cut the dough. To form long strands, first fold the dough over repeatedly and then slice the dough into even widths with a sharp knife. If you don't intend to cook the strands of pasta immediately, air dry before cooking to prevent strands from sticking to one another. Ravioli should be filled and sealed (see below) while the pasta is soft and pliable.

To store the dough. Fresh, cut, uncooked pasta dough can be kept refrigerated for two days. Freeze it if you intend to use it after that; it will keep in the freezer for several weeks. To prevent strips of pasta dough from sticking together, lightly dust them with flour and pack in plastic containers between sheets of wax paper. Frozen pasta is best when cooked frozen and not defrosted.

Food Processor Pasta Dough. Simpler and faster, processor pasta dough is very good, but when cooked it tends to be less delicate than the dough you make by hand.

Place the flour and salt in the work bowl of your food processor fitted with the double-edged steel blade. Turn the machine on and off a couple of times to evenly distribute the flour in the bowl. Break the eggs into a separate small bowl and lightly beat them, just to combine the yolks and whites. With the machine running, add the eggs in a slow, steady stream until they are all incorporated into the flour. The dough should form a ball on the blade. If the dough is too sticky, add more flour, a tablespoon at a time, and turn the machine on and off until the dough holds together in a ball. Take the dough from the machine; knead 5 to 10 minutes (as directed above); cover; and allow it to rest, unrefrigerated, at least 15 minutes before rolling it out either by hand or with a pasta machine.

Green/Spinach Pasta. Spinach can be added to the basic pasta recipe to make green pasta. Use $1/4$ cup well-drained, finely chopped cooked spinach. Add the spinach to the eggs, incorporating it into the dough as you mix in the flour with a fork. At first, the spinach in the dough appears as green flecks, but as you proceed to knead and roll out the dough, the dough becomes uniformly green in color.

Black Pepper Pasta. You can add black pepper to the basic pasta dough to make a spicy-tasting pasta. Add 1 teaspoon of finely ground black pepper to the eggs, incorporating it into the dough as you mix the flour and eggs.

Red/Tomato Pasta. Proceed with the recipe for fresh pasta, above, and add 2 tablespoons of tomato paste with the eggs, incorporating it into the dough as you mix the flour and eggs.

Hot Red Pepper Pasta. Hot red pepper gives pasta a sharp bite. Add 1 teaspoon red pepper flakes (*peperoncino*) that have been pulverized with a mortar and pestle to the eggs, incorporating it into the pasta dough as you mix the flour and eggs.

Lemon-Flavored Pasta. I love the taste of lemon pasta served cold in salads. Add 3 tablespoons of fresh lemon juice to the eggs and incorporate the juice into the dough as you mix the flour and eggs.

▓ LIGURIAN NO-EGG PASTA DOUGH

1 POUND OF DOUGH, APPROXIMATELY 4 SERVINGS

In Liguria, where pesto is supreme, fresh pasta is made without eggs—with only flour and water and sometimes a little white wine. This makes a softer dough that is not quite as flavorful and rich-tasting, but it is a bit more delicate, lighter, and really better for you. You can use this dough recipe for all the recipes that call for fresh pasta. It is particularly good with the Basil and Goat Cheese Filling for ravioli (see page 229).

About 3 cups all-purpose unbleached white flour
1 cup water
1 teaspoon kosher salt

The technique for making eggless pasta dough by hand is exactly like preparing the dough with eggs. Arrange your flour on the work surface in a ring. Place the water and salt in the center and, using a fork, beat the water in a circular motion to gradually incorporate the flour into the liquid. When the dough is soft and pliable, and not sticky, knead it on a well-floured surface for 5 minutes.

Cover with a dish towel or sheet of waxed paper and allow it to rest unrefrigerated, at least 15 minutes. Proceed with the instructions for rolling out the dough on page 9.

STORE-BOUGHT FRESH PASTA

The best substitute for homemade pasta is pasta you buy from a specialty shop selling handmade fresh pasta. If you are not fortunate enough to have access to such a store, you can find fresh pasta products in the refrigerated section of your supermarket, including *tortellini, ravioli, fettucine, linguine,* and many more. These don't measure up to homemade, but they are adequate if you're in a hurry and convenient to keep on hand in your freezer for last-minute meals. At least two big-name brands—Contadina (made by Nestlé) and DeGornio (a Kraft product)—are available in most parts of the country and in most supermarkets. Less well-known brands are found regionally. Although there are some differences, I have found all supermarket brands to be similar in quality, taste, and texture. All are pasteurized, which means that they are partially cooked; and almost all are made with eggs. Many have preservatives in them. Some eggless fresh pasta products are available, usually listed as "cholesterol free."

Another substitute for homemade fresh pasta are the prepared pasta squares sold as wonton wrappers available in oriental markets and in the refrigerated section of some supermarkets. These are good for preparing homemade ravioli (see page 221).

COOKING PASTA

When boiling dry or fresh pasta, you get the best and most reliable results if you use plenty of water and drain the pasta as soon as it is cooked through, which is usually only seconds before it is over-cooked. The point at which the pasta is done is usually referred to as *al dente*, which means "to the tooth." That point can be determined only by biting into a strand or piece of cooking pasta. (I don't go along with the doneness test of tossing a piece of pasta against the wall to see if it sticks.) Taste, I find is always the best test. At the *al dente* point, the pasta should be chewy, but not crunchy, and never soft. After biting into a piece of pasta, I look to see a pin-dot of uncooked pasta in the cross-section; then I drain it immediately. Because the pasta continues to cook even after it's drained, this ensures that the pasta will not be overcooked when it reaches the table.

All the following recipes give cooking times that span several minutes. Cooking time is determined by several factors, including the quantity of pasta and water and the temperature of the water. Always try to put the pasta into rapidly boiling water. The water will momentarily stop boiling. Start timing the pasta from the moment the water comes back to a boil after you put in the pasta. Then start testing the pasta for doneness at the earliest time given, and don't cook the pasta beyond the longer time listed. It is important that the water be at a full rolling boil when you put in the pasta—otherwise, it takes too long for the water to come back to a boil and your timing will be off.

Cooking times also vary for different pastas. Fresh pasta cooks much more quickly than dry. For example, fresh fettucine cooks in 5 minutes or less compared with dry fettucine, which takes 7 to 8 minutes. And different pasta shapes require more cooking than others. *Cappellini*, angel hair pasta, cooks in 3 to 5 minutes, whereas *orecchiette*, little ears, takes closer to 10.

Most of the recipes in this book call for one pound of pasta. For that amount of pasta, an 8-quart pot is sufficient. I highly recommend the specialized pasta pots fitted with colander inserts (which also can be used for steaming, boiling, or blanching vegetables). These are the most convenient because you can quickly and efficiently lift the pasta from the boiling water and transfer it directly to the serving bowl or the skillet with the sauce without juggling a strainer and pouring off quarts of scalding water. These pots are also very helpful if you are cooking two types of pasta because you can strain out the first pasta and reuse the heated water for the second, saving time and energy.

A wooden or plastic pasta fork, which has perpendicular dowels or claws on one side, is handy when cooking strands of pasta such as *spaghetti* or *fettucine*: it makes it easy to separate the strands while they cook and helps when sampling pasta to test for doneness. A slotted spoon is useful for cooking short pasta shapes, for stirring, and for pulling out pieces for testing doneness.

If you are not using a pasta pot with a built-in strainer, one large colander is essential for draining cooked pasta.

Always drain pasta but don't rinse it under cold or hot water. The starch adds flavor and texture to the dish. (The exception to this is pasta salads; the pasta can be rinsed in cold water to stop the cooking, see page 149.)

BASIC INSTRUCTIONS FOR COOKING PASTA

6 to 8 quarts water
1 pound pasta
1 tablespoon kosher salt

Place the water in an 8-quart stock pot. Cover and bring the water to a boil over high heat. When the water comes to a rolling boil, add the pasta and salt. Cook, uncovered, stirring frequently, until the pasta is tender but firm, *al dente*, 7 to 10 minutes. Drain the pasta using the built-in strainer in the pot or a large colander. If saucing it, transfer the pasta directly to a preheated serving bowl (or individual bowls) or to the skillet with sauce. Toss well and serve.

SERVING PASTA

Calculating precise pasta portions is not always easy. How hungry are you? Are the portions for a first course or main course? For lunch or dinner? The basic rule when it comes to figuring pasta is that 4 ounces of dry pasta and 3 ounces of fresh pasta make one average full-portion serving. The recipes in this book go along with that and typically call for a pound of pasta to serve four as a main course; six as a first course. In some recipes that combine pasta with a lot of vegetables, a half-pound of pasta serves four as a main course.

However you measure it, a simple plate of pasta and sauce will be elevated to great heights with some extra effort in serving and presentation. You have several options when it comes to serving pasta. The most festive way is to serve it is family style from a large serving bowl or platter. For more elegant affairs, serve it in individual plates or bowls with a decorative garnish. The rustic approach is to dish it out from the skillet in which you prepare the pasta sauce.

Whichever way you plan to serve the pasta, it is essential to preheat the bowl(s), plates, or platter you plan to serve it from and in—if serving from the skillet, presumably it will already be hot. Pasta cools quickly, and when placed in a cold dish, it cools even faster and loses some of its great taste. You can easily preheat dishes with the water in which the pasta cooks. Just ladle some of the boiling water into the serving dishes while the pasta is cooking. Pour it out and wipe the bowl dry before adding the cooked pasta.

The best pasta serving bowls I've found are the wide, flat, heavy ceramic bowls sold expressly for pasta. Made in Italy, some have painted patterns on them, whereas others are all white. They typically come in two sizes. The large is big enough to serve a pound of pasta and sauce. The small size serves individual portions. Their thick sides help to keep the pasta warm and their open shape is perfect for tossing the pasta with the sauce and makes a handsome serving dish to show off the pasta at its best.

At the table, serve pasta with good-quality imported Parmesan cheese (see page 23), preferably Parmigiano-Reggiano or Grana. You can serve it already grated or in a single piece with a hand-held grater for diners to grate their own. Add some good crusty bread and a fresh green salad, and your plate of pasta — presto — is an inviting and deliciously satisfying, healthful meal.

Chapter Two

THE PASTA PANTRY

What's wonderful about pasta and vegetable dishes is that all you need to prepare them is some good fresh produce, pasta, and a few basic ingredients. With dry pasta and a supply of olive oil, Parmesan cheese, fresh herbs, garlic, vinegar, and simple condiments on hand, you will always be ready to pick up the freshest vegetables that catch your eye and prepare a delicious and satisfying meal. Some recipes call for more specialty products, but with these few items in your pantry, you have everything you need to prepare most of the recipes in this book.

OLIVE OIL

Throughout the centuries, olive oil has maintained a prominent place in Italian culture, as well as in its cuisine. The Romans used olive oil for many nonculinary purposes, including fuel for their lamps, cosmetics, and as a body treatment for athletes. To the Romans, olive oil was also the *olio santo*, or sacred oil, and it was considered a healing balm for illnesses and a restorer of youth.

But it is in Italian cooking that olive oil has achieved and maintained, over thousands of years, its most significant status. Olive oil is the most important ingredient in Italian cooking and is used in the preparation of most of the recipes in this book.

The process by which olive oil is made today is essentially the same as it has been for centuries: crushing and grinding the olives, pits and all, into a coarse paste; spreading the crushed olive paste onto filters; and stacking the covered filters into a press and pressing out the oil. Although all olive oil is pressed in generally this same manner, many factors determine the quality and the flavor of the finished product.

Like wine in Italy, olive oil and its production are government-regulated and controlled, and the different oils are classified. The best olive oil, labeled *extra virgin*, has an acidity level of less than 1 percent. It is generally made from the first pressing of the highest quality olives, often hand picked (over-ripe or bruised olives raise the acidity level and lower the quality of the oil). Within the category of extra virgin oils, however, are still more distinctions and quality standards, based on such factors as whether the oil is filtered or unfiltered, cold or hot pressed, or whether any chemicals or additives are used in grinding or pressing. In addition, the size, age, location, and modernity of the *frantoio*, or oil factory, where the oil is pressed and the *oleoficio* where the oil is bottled also affect the quality and status of the oil.

In the United States, what we call *pure* olive oil is refined olive oil with a higher acidity level. Made from the second and third pressings of olives, or from the first pressing of lesser quality olives, or even from the pressing of the olive pits, pure olive oil starts out with an acidity level between 3 percent and 4 percent. Called *lampante*, it is refined in factories to remove impurities and ultimately lower the acidity level to below 3 percent. Before bottling, a small percentage of extra virgin oil is added to the refined oil to give it color and flavor. The differences among pure olive oils come primarily from the quantity and quality of extra virgin oil added to it.

When choosing olive oil, the most important factor is your own taste. I like to use three different types of oil in cooking and preparing my recipes: a light-tasting pure olive oil for most cooking; an extra virgin oil for some cooking and dressing of salads; and an unfiltered extra virgin oil for drizzling and embellishing some dishes where the flavor of the oil can really be appreciated. The oil you use for cooking should not have a particularly strong or distinctive flavor. As one respected chef in Italy told me, "Food that is cooked in oil should taste like the food, not the oil." On the other hand, the oil that you add to salads and other dishes can and should have a particular and characteristically fruity olive taste that adds to and complements the dish. When a recipe does not specify a particular type of olive oil, use your choice.

One of the easily affordable minor luxuries in the kitchen is to buy one or two small bottles of fine extra virgin olive oil, such as the Raineri *Prela* from Liguria, with its almost sweet taste, or the Badia a Coltibuono from Tuscany, with its peppery, fruity flavor, and to explore the differences they offer; then pick your own favorite.

Olive oil will keep for many months in a cool, dark place. An unopened container can keep for as long as two years. If you buy the oil by the gallon, you should transfer a small quantity—a quart or a liter of oil—to a serving container for daily use.

PARMESAN CHEESE

Cheese is an indispensable ingredient in the preparation of many pasta dishes. Over the centuries, numerous cheeses have been developed throughout Italy—both the soft, fresh varieties without rinds as well as many aged, hard-rind cheeses. The ancient Greeks first brought cheese to the Italian peninsula and taught the Etruscans how to take the curds from sour milk and form them into cheeses. The Etruscans took the process a step farther and developed hard-rind cheese, similar to what eventually became known as Parmesan cheese, which was aged and lasted much longer than the soft, fresh cheeses. The Romans were the first to use rennet (the lining from a milk-fed calf's stomach) to induce the curdling process of the milk—before then milk was left to sour naturally. In his book, *Rei Rusticae (On Rustic Matters*, A.D. 65), Columella, a Roman writer and agriculturalist, recorded the cheese-making process of his day, which does not differ significantly from the process today.

The most important Italian cheese—the one most used in cooking and serving pasta—is Parmesan. The two basic types of Italian Parmesan are Parmigiano-Reggiano and Grana. The best is indisputably the Parmigiano-Reggiano. It is a strictly controlled hand-made product that has been produced continuously in the same manner for over 700 years in small *caseifici*, cheese factories, and only in a narrowly defined area around Parma, Reggio-Emilia, Modena, Bologna, and Mantova. Grana has a taste and texture similar to Parmigiano-Reggiano but is made mostly in large factories located primarily in Lombardy and Piedmont and is produced in much bigger quantities and with fewer controls and restrictions.

Unlike other cheeses in Italy that have succumbed to modern industrial techniques, Parmigiano-Reggiano is produced today the way it has been produced for centuries, although modern equipment is used in the process: Milk comes from local cows that feed only on fresh grass; gathered from two milkings a day, the milk is partially skimmed and augmented with whey from the previous day's milkings to encourage fermentation. The cheese is curdled with rennet, still a natural product from calves. The curds are formed into wheels and air dried, which causes the rind to form, then soaked in heavily salted water, which both preserves and flavors the cheese. The end products are 60- to 70-pound wheels of cheese—each bearing its production date and the Parmigiano-Reggiano logo—that are then aged from 18 months to two years, although the younger, moister wheels of Parmigiano-Reggiano cheeses are generally considered to be better. You can always identify real Parmigiano-Reggiano cheese by the distinctive imprint stamped on the yellow rind. Parmigiano-Reggiano has a nutty, mild flavor and is only slightly salty.

Grana is made under less stringent guidelines than Parmigiano-Reggiano and is, therefore, generally less expensive. Its flavor, although still relatively mild and nutty tasting, is slightly sharper than that of Parmigiano-Reggiano and more salty. However, its texture is very similar to that of Parmigiano-Reggiano, and the two cheeses can be used interchangeably in most recipes calling for Parmesan. There are several types of Grana, but in the United States Grana Padano (*Padano* meaning *from the Po River*) from Piedmont and Lombardy is most often available. Grana Lodigiano is from the town of Lodi in southern Lombardy, and Grana Piacentino is from the town of Piacenza, also in Lombardy.

Parmesan-type cheeses also come from other countries, including Argentina and the United States. I would only recommend these if Italian varieties are not available.

Whether you buy Parmigiano-Reggiano or Grana, you should buy it by the piece and grate it just before you are ready to use it. Ground Parmesan takes on a sour flavor—even in the refrigerator—after about a week. A chunk of Parmesan, on the other hand, keeps in the refrigerator for months if wrapped securely and kept airtight.

When you buy Parmesan by the piece, you must grate it yourself when you want to use it. You can easily grate Parmesan in a food processor; although I don't particularly like the powdery texture this method produces, it is fast and efficient, especially if you are using the cheese to cook with rather than serve it at the table. For serving Parmesan at the table, I find that hand-grating adds to the pleasure of the meal, and at our table we grate the Parmesan on a small, fine, single-sided handheld grater. When many people are at the table, it takes too long for the cheese to make its way around before the pasta turns cold, so for those times, pregrated cheese is in order. For grating large quantities of cheese, I prefer to use a rotary hand-grater, such as a Mouli, which quickly and easily grates the cheese to the proper consistency. (Mouli graters are widely available in hardware and specialty cookware shops.)

Another implement for cheese is the Parmesan knife. In Italy, different knives are used for practically every type of cheese, but none is more distinctive than the spear-shaped blade of the Parmesan knife. The blades can range in size from 2 to about 6 inches long, but all have stubby round handles. Parmesan is meant to be broken, not cut, into uneven pieces. The Parmesan knife works as a wedge to break off the shards. In lieu of a Parmesan knife, which is available from Williams-Sonoma and other specialty food and tool shops, you can use a clam knife. Just dig the blade into the cheese and pull off a piece.

Several recipes in the book call for shaved Parmesan. A good old-fashioned vegetable peeler does the job very well. You also can use the single blade on a standard four-sided grater or a special truffle grater with an adjustable blade, available from specialty knife stores.

VINEGAR

Wine vinegar, a byproduct of the great Italian wine-making industry, is made everywhere wine is made in Italy and usually from good red and white wines. The best wine vinegars are made in wooden barrels. White wine vinegar should have a pale pinkish color, whereas red wine vinegar can range in color from pink to deep, dark red. Good wine vinegars are always transparent.

In contrast, balsamic vinegar, with its sweet and sour flavor, thick, syrupy texture, and rich, dark brown color, is a vinegar in a league by itself. Since the Middle Ages, it has been made in the area around Modena, in the region of Reggio-Emilia, from the cooked and concentrated juice of white Trebbiano grapes that is aged in progressively smaller wooden barrels. Like extra virgin olive oil and Parmigiano-Reggiano cheese, the production of balsamic vinegar is controlled by law. The real product carries the label *aceto balsamico tradizionale*. To be labeled that way, it must have been aged at least 12 years and sometimes as many as 50 years or more. Those products sold as balsamic vinegar without the official label either have not been aged as long or are imitations: red wine vinegar that has been flavored with caramel. The difference among the vinegars is in the flavor and the price. The *tradizionale* can cost as much as $40 for a 100-gram bottle; other versions are comparably less expensive.

Even though the flavor of balsamic vinegar is not as sharp as that of regular wine vinegar, use only a small quantity in recipes because it can easily overpower the flavor of the dish.

HERBS

When it comes to cooking pasta, fresh, rather than dried, herbs should be used whenever possible. The flavor of dried herbs, because it is concentrated, is usually stronger if not altogether different from that of the fresh variety. To substitute, the general rule is for every tablespoon of fresh herbs, use 1 teaspoon dried. If a particular fresh herb is not available, I often substitute fresh parsley because it is generally available year-round everywhere, rather than use the dried herbs; although the flavor is not the same, you get a fresh-tasting dish.

Storage of fresh herbs varies, depending on the herb. Most can be kept for at least several days in the refrigerator if wrapped in a paper towel and stored in a plastic bag. You also can freeze or dry most fresh herbs, but you won't get the same intensity of flavor that you get when you use them fresh. As long as weather permits, it's nice to keep a few pots of fresh herbs growing on your back porch, on your windowsill, or in your garden.

Basil. More than any other herb, basil is associated with Italian cooking. It is the essential ingredient in many Ligurian dishes, most notably pesto; and throughout all the regions of Italy, basil is a fundamental component of pasta sauces, soups, and salads. The basil plant is an annual and a member of the mint family, with leaves that can be broad or tiny, green or dark purple. It is available—in less or more abundance—throughout most of the year. Cut basil is perishable and should be purchased the day you intend to use it and thoroughly washed and dried just before cooking. Although basil readily wilts and turns brown in the refrigerator from both the cold and the moisture, you can extend its vitality if, before you wash it, you wrap it in paper towels, put it in a plastic bag, and place it in the crisper of your refrigerator.

Parsley. The flatleaf, so-called Italian parsley is widely used in the preparation of pasta and vegetable dishes throughout Italy. It is almost always used in cooking, rather than added for decoration. Parsley is high in nutrients, particularly vitamins C and A as well as potassium, iron, and calcium. The ancient Romans sometimes wore garlands of parsley around their heads and necks, supposedly to fend off drunkenness. Parsley can be washed and kept for up to a week in the refrigerator. For convenience, you can chop parsley and keep it uncovered in a dish in the refrigerator for several days; after that it begins to dry out and lose its flavor.

Red Pepper Flakes. Dried hot red pepper flakes (called *peperoncino* in Italy), the dried seeds from hot red chili peppers, are added to many dishes in the southern regions of Italy. The *arrabbiata* sauce of Abruzzi is typically seasoned with *peperoncino*, as is the classic pasta *aglio e olio*, with garlic and oil. *Peperoncino* is also added to olive oil used to dress salads or for cooking, to infuse it with flavor. Because you use only a pinch of *peperoncino* at a time, one container can last for years, but you may find that the flavor wanes over time and that the flakes lose some of their spark. Invest in some new pepper flakes at least once a year.

Garlic. Once used for purely medicinal purposes, garlic remains one of the essential ingredients in Italian cooking. Heads of garlic should be firm to the touch when you buy them. As they age, the bulbs dry out; the cloves turn brown; and the paperlike skin starts to flake away. Always store garlic in a dry, preferably cool place. Freshly picked young heads of garlic tend to be less pungent than older heads of garlic that have been stored for several months.

The best way to peel a clove of garlic is to use a sharp paring knife and cut away the root end of the clove. The skin on the clove usually comes away easily after that. If you're in a hurry, place the unpeeled garlic clove between your kitchen counter and the flat side of a large chef's knife — the sharp edge away from you. Pound the knife blade bluntly with the side of your fist. The garlic clove should flatten slightly and separate from the skin.

Most of the recipes in this book that use garlic call for it to be finely minced or pressed, which means you can either chop the garlic, with a knife or in a food processor, or force it through a garlic press, depending on whether or not you want to have actual pieces of garlic in the dish you are preparing. Some garlic purists may tell you that any way of chopping garlic except with a knife renders the clove bitter. I usually can't taste the difference.

When cooking with garlic, be careful not to burn or overly brown it, which gives a distinctive, unpleasant, bitter taste. It is possible to flavor food with garlic without leaving a trace of garlic clove in the dish. Heat a whole, peeled clove of garlic in the oil to be used for cooking until the clove turns a golden color. Remove the garlic and discard it. You can use this garlic-flavored oil to baste vegetables before roasting or grilling.

Salt. I like to use kosher salt, with its large, coarse crystals in cooking; it is pure salt, unlike the iodized varieties, which contain additives. The quantities for salt listed in the recipes in this book are approximate and given as "salt to taste." And I mean just that: always taste before salting and add only as much as you find necessary.

Pepper. Whenever pepper is called for, unless otherwise specified, use freshly ground black pepper.

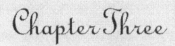

Chapter Three

PASTA AND VEGETABLE SAUCES

Great vegetable sauces for pasta call for great produce. You have to choose the best of what's available—which means you may not always come home with what you went to the store to buy—and then cook the vegetables in a way that heightens and enhances their delicious natural taste. Vegetables prepared for pasta sauce should have enough flavor to be served on their own. As in Italy, the main ingredients should be able to speak for themselves.

Great sauces also depend on choosing a pasta shape that *fits* the sauce. Although pasta shapes are easily interchangeable, some informal guidelines are helpful: tomato sauces, *ragùs* (meat and tomato sauces), and creamy sauces typically go with pasta strands such as spaghetti, linguine, or fettucine; chunky pasta sauces with pieces of vegetables should be paired with short pasta shapes like *penne* (quills), *fusilli* (squiggles), and *farfalle* (bow ties)—shapes that catch vegetable pieces and allow you to pick them up easily with your fork. Dried beans go with very short shapes such as *tubetti* (short macaroni) or *conchigliette* (little shells). Cheese sauces are like tomato sauces and are usually paired with the wider strands like *fettucine* or the widest, *pappardelle*. Always use pasta made from 100 percent durum wheat (see page 4), and cook it to just the *al dente* point: slightly chewy, but tender all the way through. These recipes call for the most readily available, popular pasta shapes. With hundreds of different pasta shapes to choose from, feel free, within these guidelines, to substitute.

✳ SPAGHETTI PRIMAVERA

6 SERVINGS

This pasta and vegetable dish was created by Sirio Maccioni, the owner of the New York Restaurant Le Cirque.

1 bunch broccoli, heavy stalks discarded and tops cut into
    bite-size florets
2 small zucchini, ends discarded, cut into quarters lengthwise,
    and each quarter cut into 1-inch pieces
4 asparagus spears, tough bottoms discarded and spears cut
    into 3 pieces
1½ cups 1-inch pieces green beans
1 tablespoon kosher salt, plus extra for cooking vegetables
    and seasoning
½ cup fresh or frozen peas
2 pounds ripe plum tomatoes
¼ cup plus 2 tablespoons olive oil
2 cups thinly sliced mushrooms
Freshly ground black pepper
1 teaspoon finely chopped fresh hot red or green chili pepper
    or about ½ teaspoon dried red pepper flakes
¼ cup finely chopped fresh parsley leaves
2 cloves garlic, pressed or finely minced
6 fresh basil leaves, chopped, or about 1 teaspoon dried basil
⅔ cup pine nuts
1 pound dry spaghetti or spaghettini
¼ cup (½ stick) unsalted butter
2 tablespoons broth (see pages 121–26)
About ½ cup heavy cream
⅔ cup freshly grated Parmesan cheese

Cook the broccoli, zucchini, asparagus, and green beans separately in boiling salted water until tender, but still crisp, about 5 minutes. Drain well; run cold water over them to stop the cooking and drain again; combine in a mixing bowl. Cook the peas for 1 minute in boiling salted water if fresh and 30 seconds if frozen. Drain; run under cold water and drain again; combine with the other vegetables.

Add the tomatoes to the boiling water and cook exactly 1 minute. Drain. Cut out the seeds and cores and peel off the skins. Coarsely chop the tomatoes (to yield approximately 3 cups).

Heat ¼ cup of the olive oil in a large skillet over medium-high heat and add the mushrooms. Season with salt and pepper to taste. Cook, stirring, about 2 minutes. Add the hot pepper and parsley; cook 1 minute longer. Add half the garlic and all of the tomatoes and season with salt and pepper to taste. Cook, stirring gently, about 10 minutes longer. Stir in the basil and set aside.

Heat the remaining 2 tablespoons of olive oil in a large skillet over medium-high heat with the remaining garlic and the green vegetable mixture. Cook just long enough to heat the vegetables through, 2 to 3 minutes. Do not overcook. Turn off the heat and set aside.

Put the pine nuts in a small skillet. Place over medium heat; cook, stirring constantly until they are brown, about 5 minutes. Transfer to a small dish.

Meanwhile, bring a large pot of water to a rolling boil over high heat. Add the tablespoon of salt and the spaghetti. Cook, stirring occasionally, until the pasta is tender but firm, *al dente*, 7 to 10 minutes. Drain. In the pot in which the spaghetti cooked, combine the butter, broth, cream, and Parmesan. Cook over medium heat until the mixture is thick and smooth, 3 to 5 minutes. Reduce the heat to low; add the spaghetti and toss quickly to blend. Add the vegetables and any liquid from them and toss until the mixture is combined and the liquids thickened. The sauce should not be soupy. Serve in individual preheated serving bowls. Garnish with pine nuts.

⊞ PASTA PRIMAVERA LA CHIUSA

4 SERVINGS

Pasta Primavera has found its way from the Le Cirque restaurant where it was created into so many kitchens that there are probably as many variations now as there are cooks. This variation comes from the restaurant/inn La Chiusa in Tuscany. Feel free to improvise with whatever vegetables are fresh at the market, keeping the quantities approximately the same.

6 tablespoons ($^3/_4$ stick) unsalted butter

1 tablespoon finely chopped scallion (white part only) or shallot

1 small zucchini, ends discarded and cut into fine julienne strips

1 small summer squash, ends discarded and cut into fine julienne strips

1 cup packed fresh spinach leaves, rinsed well in several changes of cold water, drained, stems removed, and finely chopped

6 fresh squash blossoms, stamens and pistels removed, shredded (optional, if available)

1 tablespoon chopped fresh basil leaves

1 tablespoon kosher salt, plus extra for seasoning

Freshly ground black pepper

$^1/_2$ pound fresh egg fettucine

$^1/_4$ cup chopped fresh chives

$^1/_2$ cup freshly grated Parmesan cheese, plus more for serving

Heat the butter in a large skillet over medium-high heat until bubbly. Add the scallion and cook, stirring, 1 minute. Add the zucchini, summer squash, spinach, squash blossoms, and basil; season with salt and pepper to taste. Cook, stirring, until the zucchini is tender, 5 to 7 minutes. Turn off the heat and set aside.

Bring a large pot of water to a rolling boil over high heat. Add a tablespoon of salt and the fettucine; cook, stirring occasionally, until the pasta is tender but firm, *al dente*, about 5 minutes. Drain well and transfer to the sauté pan with the vegetables. Turn the heat to low. Add the chives and Parmesan; toss until the pasta and vegetables are combined and the liquid is thickened. Serve immediately.

SPAGHETTI WITH BABY STRING BEANS, ARUGULA, AND WATERCRESS SAUCE

4 TO 6 SERVINGS

This pesto-like sauce of bitter greens has a mildly sharp taste and is surprisingly light. You can use it on any pasta shape, but I like it best with spaghetti and baby string beans—haricot verts are the best if they're available. This recipe was inspired by a dish I enjoyed in Tuscany made of fresh fettucine, pesto, and the deliciously tender Sant' Anna *fagiolini* green beans.

1 cup packed arugula leaves, stems cut off and discarded and
      leaves rinsed in several changes of cold water
1 cup packed watercress leaves, thickest bottom stems discarded
      and leaves rinsed in several changes of cold water
1 large clove garlic, peeled
2 tablespoons pine nuts
1 tablespoon kosher salt, plus extra for seasoning
$^{1}/_{2}$ cup olive oil
1 pound dry spaghetti
$^{1}/_{2}$ pound smallest string beans or haricot verts, tips cut off and
      discarded
Freshly grated Parmesan cheese

In a food processor fitted with a metal blade, combine the arugula, watercress, garlic, pine nuts, and salt to taste. Process until finely chopped, about 10 seconds. With the machine running, slowly add the oil and process until the sauce is smooth. Scrape the sides down with a rubber spatula and process a few seconds longer. Set aside.

Bring a large pot of water to a rolling boil over high heat. Add the tablespoon of salt and the spaghetti. Cook, stirring occasionally, 3 minutes. Add the string beans and cook until the string beans and pasta are tender but firm, *al dente*, 4 to 5 minutes longer. Drain; transfer to a preheated large serving bowl. Pour the arugula and watercress sauce over the spaghetti and string beans. Toss well; serve with Parmesan.

LINGUINE FINI WITH FRESH ARUGULA AND ROASTED YELLOW PEPPER SAUCE

4 TO 6 SERVINGS

The brilliant yellow and green colors of this dish make a beautiful presentation. The sweetness of the yellow peppers is deliciously contrasted by the sharp, peppery taste of the arugula.

2 large yellow bell peppers (about 1 1/2 pounds)
1/4 cup olive oil
1 clove garlic, pressed or finely minced
1 tablespoon mascarpone cheese
1 tablespoon kosher salt, plus extra for seasoning
1 pound dry linguine fini or spaghettini
Freshly ground black pepper
1 bunch arugula, thick stems cut off and discarded, leaves rinsed
    in several changes of cold water, dried and coarsely chopped
    (to yield about 2 cups)
Freshly grated Parmesan cheese

Preheat the oven broiler. Cut the peppers in half lengthwise and remove the core and seeds. Place the pepper halves cut side down on a baking sheet covered with aluminum foil. Place the peppers under the broiler about 6 inches from the heat and broil until completely black, about 8 minutes. Remove from the oven, cover loosely with foil, and allow to stand for 10 minutes. Under cold running water, peel the skins from the peppers. They should come off easily. Place the peeled peppers in a food processor or blender and process until smooth.

Heat the oil in a medium-size skillet over medium heat. Add the garlic and pepper puree; cook, stirring, until the oil and peppers are thoroughly combined, about 5 minutes. Stir in the mascarpone with a wire whisk. Season with salt and pepper to taste and set aside. Reheat gently before combining with the pasta.

Bring a large pot of water to a rolling boil over high heat. Add the tablespoon of salt and the linguine. Cook, stirring occasionally, until the pasta is tender but firm, *al dente*, 7 to 10 minutes. Drain; transfer to a large preheated serving bowl. Add the yellow pepper sauce and arugula leaves to the pasta. Toss well; serve with Parmesan.

PENNE WITH ROASTED ASPARAGUS AND SHAVED GRANA

4 SERVINGS

I learned about roasting asparagus from Johanne Killeen, co-owner and co-chef with her husband, George Germon, of the Providence, Rhode Island, restaurant Al Forno. Roasting intensifies the flavor of the asparagus and makes it taste so good you'll wonder why you ever cooked it any other way. This dish calls for Grana, which is a type of Parmesan cheese made in Lombardy in

Italy (see page 24). It is a wonderful, tangy-tasting cheese and less expensive than Parmigiano-Reggiano.

1 pound thin asparagus spears, tough bottoms discarded and
  spears cut diagonally into 2-inch pieces, leaving the tips intact
1/4 cup olive oil
1 large clove garlic, thinly sliced
1 tablespoon kosher salt, plus extra for sprinkling
1/2 pound dry penne
3 ounces Grana Parmesan cheese (in a single piece)

Preheat the oven to 500°F. Place the asparagus pieces in a small roasting pan with the oil and garlic; stir well to coat with the oil. Sprinkle lightly with salt. Roast on the topmost rack in the oven for 10 to 15 minutes until brown. Remove from the oven and set aside.

Meanwhile, bring a large pot of water to a rolling boil over high heat. Add the tablespoon of salt and the penne. Cook, stirring occasionally, until the pasta is tender but firm, *al dente*, 7 to 10 minutes. Drain; transfer to a large preheated serving bowl. Add the roasted asparagus and toss well to combine. Use a vegetable peeler to shave the Grana over the pasta. Toss and serve.

PENNE WITH ARTICHOKES, LEMON, AND CAPERS

4 SERVINGS

The artichokes combine with the capers and lemon to make an invitingly tangy dish with a refreshing taste.

3 medium-size fresh artichokes (about 1 $\frac{1}{2}$ pounds)

$\frac{1}{4}$ cup olive oil

1 clove garlic, pressed or finely minced

1 tablespoon kosher salt, plus extra for seasoning

Juice of $\frac{1}{2}$ lemon

$\frac{1}{2}$ cup water

$\frac{1}{2}$ pound dry penne

1 tablespoon small capers, drained

2 tablespoons chopped fresh parsley leaves

$\frac{1}{4}$ cup freshly grated Parmigiano-Reggiano or other Parmesan
  cheese, plus more for serving

Peel away the tough dark green leaves on each artichoke. Starting with the leaves closest to the stem, break off the leaves all around the artichoke until only the yellow-green leaves are visible. Do not use scissors or a knife for this; the leaves will break naturally at the point where the tough part ends and the tender part begins. Use a serrated knife to cut 1 to 2 inches off the top of the artichoke; use a small paring knife to peel the stem and trim around the base. Cut the artichoke in quarters lengthwise. Cut out the choke on each quarter. Thinly slice the artichokes lengthwise (to yield about 4 cups).

Heat the oil in a medium-size nonaluminum skillet over medium-high heat. Add the garlic, artichokes, and salt to taste; cook, stirring, 1 to 2 minutes. Add the lemon juice and water and bring to a boil. Reduce the heat to medium-low; cover and simmer until the artichokes are tender and the water has mostly cooked away, about 20 minutes.

Bring a large pot of water to a rolling boil over high heat. Add the tablespoon of salt and the penne. Cook, stirring occasionally, until the pasta is tender but firm, *al dente*, 7 to 10 minutes. Drain;

transfer to a large preheated serving bowl. Add the artichokes, capers, parsley, and Parmesan; toss well. Serve immediately.

✦ BOW TIES WITH ARTICHOKES, POTATOES, AND FRESH SPINACH

4 SERVINGS

This dish is a gratifying main course. The combination of artichokes and potatoes is hearty enough to satisfy any appetite. The spinach gives fresh-tasting flavor.

3 medium-size fresh artichokes (about 1½ pounds)
¼ cup plus 2 tablespoons olive oil
2 small cloves garlic, pressed or finely minced
½ pound boiling potatoes, preferably Yukon Gold, peeled and cut into julienne strips (to yield about 1½ cups sliced)
1 tablespoon kosher salt, plus extra for seasoning
1 cup water
4 cups fresh spinach leaves, rinsed well in several changes of cold water, stems removed, and coarsely chopped
½ pound dry bow ties
Freshly grated Parmesan cheese

Peel away the tough dark green leaves on each artichoke. Starting with the leaves closest to the stem, break off the leaves all around the artichoke until only the yellow-green leaves are visible. Do not use scissors or a knife for this; the leaves will break naturally at the point where the tough part ends and the tender part begins. Use a serrated knife to cut 1 to 2 inches off the top of the artichoke; use a small paring knife to peel the stem and trim around the base. Cut the artichoke in quarters lengthwise. Cut out the fuzzy choke on each quarter. Thinly slice the artichokes lengthwise (to yield about 4 cups).

Heat ¼ cup of the olive oil in a medium-size nonaluminum skillet over medium heat and add 1 clove of the garlic and the potatoes. Cook, stirring, about 2 minutes. Add the artichokes to the skillet. Season with salt to taste. Cook, stirring, until the artichokes begin to soften slightly, about 2 minutes. Add the water, bring to a boil, and cover. Reduce heat to medium-low and simmer until the artichokes and potatoes are tender and the water is mostly evaporated, about 20 minutes. You can prepare this several hours ahead of time and reheat just before serving.

Heat the remaining oil in a small skillet over medium-high heat. Add the remaining garlic and the spinach; season lightly with salt. Cook, stirring, until the spinach is wilted and tender, about 5 minutes.

Meanwhile, bring a large pot of water to a rolling boil over high heat. Add the tablespoon of salt and the bow ties. Cook, stirring occasionally, until the pasta is tender but firm, *al dente*, 7 to 10 minutes. Drain; transfer to a preheated serving dish. Add the artichokes, potatoes, and spinach; toss well. Serve with Parmesan.

ABOUT ARTICHOKES

Artichokes are available in the United States throughout the year but are considered in season in the late fall and early spring. The smallest artichokes, *carciofini,* as they are called in Italy, are about the size of a jumbo-size egg and are the only artichokes you can eat raw; medium-size artichokes are about 3 to 4 inches tall; large artichokes are 5 to 6 inches high. To store artichokes, wrap them in plastic and refrigerate; otherwise, they dry out and lose their flavor.

PENNE WITH BROCCOLI, CAULIFLOWER, AND TOASTED BREAD CRUMBS

4 TO 6 SERVINGS

This recipe was inspired by a dish I enjoyed at Chez Panisse in Berkeley, California, where the baby-size vegetables come from the Chino Ranch organic farm near San Diego. Happily, ordinary produce also yields delicious results.

1 bunch of broccoli, heavy stalks discarded and tops cut
   into bite-size florets
1 cup bite-size cauliflower florets
1/4 cup plus 2 tablespoons olive oil
1 clove garlic, pressed or finely minced
1 small red onion, cut in half and very thinly sliced
1 tablespoon kosher salt, plus extra for seasoning
1 1/4 cups unseasoned bread crumbs
1 pound dry penne
Freshly grated Parmesan cheese

Place the broccoli and cauliflower florets in a small mixing bowl with cold water to cover and let soak 30 minutes to release any sand or dirt in them. Drain; set aside. Bring a small saucepan of water to boil over high heat. Add the broccoli and cauliflower; cook exactly 1 minute. Drain; rinse under cold water to stop the cooking. Drain again.

Heat 1/4 cup of the olive oil in a medium-size skillet over medium-high heat. Add the garlic and onion; cook until the onion begins to soften, 2 to 3 minutes. Add the broccoli and cauliflower and season with salt to taste; cook until the florets are tender, about 3 to 5 minutes longer. Turn off the heat and set aside.

Heat the remaining 2 tablespoons of the olive oil in a small skillet over medium heat. Add the bread crumbs and mix well with a fork to thoroughly combine. Cook, stirring frequently to prevent burning, until the bread crumbs are lightly brown and toasted, about 5 minutes. Turn off the heat and set aside.

Meanwhile, bring a large pot of water to a rolling boil over high heat. Add the tablespoon of salt and the penne. Cook, stirring occasionally, until the penne is tender but firm, *al dente*, 7 to 10 minutes. Drain; transfer to a large preheated serving bowl. Add the vegetables to the pasta and toss well. Top with the bread crumbs; serve immediately with grated Parmesan.

▦ SHELLS WITH TWO BROCCOLIS, GARLIC, AND HOT RED PEPPER

4 SERVINGS

In Italy, there are many varieties of broccoli, including some that are very much like what we know as cauliflower. This recipe is my variation on a traditional southern Italian dish for pasta and broccoli. I've added the bitter, leafy broccoli rabe for a contrast in flavor that makes a delicious play on the palate.

1 cup broccoli rabe florets, cut from 1 bunch broccoli rabe, stalks and leaves discarded
1 bunch broccoli, heavy stalks discarded and tops cut into bite-size florets
1/4 cup olive oil
2 cloves garlic, pressed or finely minced
1/4 teaspoon hot red pepper flakes
1 tablespoon kosher salt, plus extra for seasoning
1/2 pound dry small pasta shells
Freshly grated Parmesan cheese

Place all the broccoli florets in a bowl with cold water to cover and allow to soak at least 30 minutes to release any sand or dirt in them. Drain.

Heat the oil in a medium-size skillet over medium-high heat. Add the garlic, hot pepper flakes, and both broccolis; season with salt to taste. Cook, stirring, until the broccoli is just tender and still bright green, about 7 minutes. Be careful not to overcook the broccoli, or it will turn an unappetizing brownish green. Turn off the heat and set aside.

Meanwhile, bring a large pot of water to a rolling boil over high heat. Add the tablespoon of salt and the shells. Cook, stirring occasionally, until the pasta is tender but firm, *al dente*, 7 to 10 minutes. Drain; transfer to a large preheated serving bowl. Add the broccoli; toss well. Serve with Parmesan.

✳ PENNE WITH WHITE BEANS, POTATOES, AND TOMATOES

4 SERVINGS

Pasta, potatoes, and beans may seem like carbohydrate overload, but this mixture makes a surprisingly light-tasting yet very flavorful and satisfying dish.

1/3 cup olive oil

2 medium-size boiling potatoes, preferably Yukon Gold, peeled and sliced into 1/4-inch julienne strips

1 cup dry white kidney beans, cooked according to the directions on pages 127–29 or one 16-ounce can cannellini beans, drained and rinsed well

1 large clove garlic, pressed or finely minced

2 fresh plum tomatoes, seeded, chopped, and combined with 1 tablespoon olive oil

1 tablespoon kosher salt, plus extra for seasoning

1/2 pound dry penne

2 tablespoons chopped fresh basil leaves

Freshly grated Parmesan cheese

Heat the olive oil in a medium-size skillet over medium-high heat. Add the potatoes; cook until the potatoes are tender but still firm and not brown, about 5 minutes. Add the beans and garlic; cook until the beans are heated through, 1 to 2 minutes longer. Add the tomatoes to the mixture and cook only another minute. Season with salt to taste. Turn off the heat and set aside.

Meanwhile, bring a large pot of water to a rolling boil over high heat. Add the tablespoon of salt and the penne. Cook, stirring occasionally, until the pasta is tender but firm, *al dente*, 7 to 10 minutes. Drain; transfer to a preheated serving bowl. Add the potato-and-bean mixture and basil; toss well to combine. Serve with Parmesan.

SPAGHETTI WITH GARLIC, HOT RED PEPPER, AND PARSLEY

4 TO 6 SERVINGS

This classic southern Italian dish is one of my all-time favorites. I usually have the ingredients on hand and find it's the perfect dish to prepare when I come home to a near-empty refrigerator. I like to use thicker spaghetti, but you can also use spaghettini or linguine with excellent results.

1 pound dry spaghetti
1 tablespoon kosher salt, plus extra for seasoning
1/4 cup olive oil
2 cloves garlic, peeled
1/4 teaspoon hot red pepper flakes
1/4 cup chopped fresh parsley leaves
Freshly grated pecorino romano cheese

Bring a large pot of water to a rolling boil over high heat. Add the spaghetti and the tablespoon of salt. Cook, stirring occasionally, until the pasta is tender but firm, *al dente*, 7 to 10 minutes. Drain.

Meanwhile, heat the oil in a large skillet with the cloves of garlic. When the cloves turn golden brown, remove and discard them. Add the hot red pepper flakes to the oil and turn off the heat. Add the cooked pasta to the pan with the parsley and toss well. Season with salt to taste. Serve with pecorino romano.

Pecorino is the generic name for Italian cheeses made with ewe's (sheep's) milk and the rennet from the stomach of the milk-fed baby lamb, *abbacchio*, which is a Roman delicacy. The aged pecorino cheeses are made throughout the central and southern regions of Italy—the sardo from Sardinia and romano from Rome.

Pecorini are aged from 2 weeks (for the sardo) to 8 months (for the romano). They are all typically very salty and sharp tasting. The longer these cheeses are aged, the better they are for grating. That is why pecorino romano cheese is often used as a substitute for Parmesan. Pecorino toscano, a soft-textured strong-flavored cheese, is a product of Tuscany.

LINGUINE WITH FRESH FENNEL, ENDIVE, AND SPINACH

4 SERVINGS

Fresh fennel and endive are sautéed with garlic for a long time until the flavors are intense and concentrated. The spinach gives the dish a great fresh taste. Slice the fennel as thinly as possible, preferably on a mandoline or in a food processor fitted with the slicing disc.

$^1\!/_2$ cup olive oil

2 cloves garlic, pressed or finely minced

1 large fennel bulb (about 1 $^1\!/_2$ pounds), tall stalks and leaves
  discarded (or reserved for another use), bulb cut in half
  lengthwise and very thinly sliced (to yield 4 cups)

2 endive, cut in half lengthwise, and cut crosswise into
  $^1\!/_4$-inch slices

1 tablespoon kosher salt, plus extra for seasoning

3 cups fresh spinach leaves, stems removed, rinsed
  well in several changes of cold water, dried, and roughly
  chopped

1 pound dry linguine or spaghetti

$^1\!/_3$ cup freshly grated Parmesan cheese, plus extra for serving

Heat the oil in a large skillet over medium-high heat. Add the garlic, fennel, and endive and season with salt to taste. Cook, stirring, until the vegetables begin to soften, about 2 minutes. Reduce the heat to low; cook, stirring occasionally, until the fennel and endive are just beginning to brown, 20 to 25 minutes. (You can prepare the fennel and endive several hours in advance to this point.) Just before serving, turn the heat to medium, reheat the fennel, and add the spinach; cook, stirring, until the spinach is tender, about 5 minutes longer.

Meanwhile, bring a large pot of water to a rolling boil over high heat. Add the linguine and the tablespoon of salt. Cook, stirring occasionally, until the pasta is tender but firm, *al dente*, 7 to 10 minutes. Drain; transfer to a large preheated serving bowl. Add the fennel, endive, and spinach sauce and the Parmesan; toss well to combine. Season with salt to taste and serve immediately.

FETTUCINE WITH CARAMELIZED LEEKS, RED ONION, AND WATERCRESS

4 TO 6 SERVINGS

The caramelized leeks and onions have an intensely rich, almost sweet flavor that is perfectly offset by the lightly cooked fresh watercress. I like this sauce with fettucine, but you can also serve it with short pasta shapes; bow ties are particularly good.

1/3 cup olive oil
1 clove garlic, pressed or finely minced
3 medium-size leeks (white part only), cut in half lengthwise, rinsed well between the layers to remove any sand or dirt, and cut lengthwise into 2-inch-long julienne strips
1 large red onion, peeled, cut in half and thinly sliced (to yield 2 cups)
1 tablespoon kosher salt, plus extra for seasoning
1 bunch watercress, thickest stems discarded, leaves rinsed well, dried, and coarsely chopped
1 pound dry fettucine
Freshly grated Parmesan cheese

Heat the oil in a medium-size skillet over medium heat. Add the garlic, leeks, and onion; season with salt to taste. Cook, stirring occasionally, until the leeks and onion are golden, about 20 minutes. If necessary, reduce the heat to low to prevent the leeks and onions from becoming overly brown too quickly. Add the watercress and cook until wilted and tender, 2 to 3 minutes longer. Turn off the heat and set aside.

Meanwhile, bring a large pot of water to a rolling boil over high heat. Add the tablespoon of salt and the fettucine. Cook, stirring occasionally, until the pasta is tender but firm, *al dente*, 7 to 10 minutes. Drain; divide the pasta into preheated individual serving bowls. Top each serving with some of the leek, onion, and watercress mixture. Serve with Parmesan.

SPAGHETTI WITH CARAMELIZED ONIONS AND FRESH HOT PEPPER

4 TO 6 SERVINGS

This recipe was inspired by a dish I enjoyed at the Milanese restaurant Aimo e Nadia. If you're unsure about the heat of your fresh hot pepper, omit it and substitute a hefty pinch of dry hot pepper flakes. Always wash your hands, knife, and cutting board thoroughly after working with fresh hot peppers.

$^1\!/_3$ cup olive oil
1 clove garlic, peeled
2 medium-size sweet onions, preferably Vidalia, peeled and sliced
    into $^1\!/_4$-inch thick rounds
1 tablespoon kosher salt, plus extra for seasoning
1 small red jalapeño or serrano pepper, stem and seeds removed
    and very finely chopped
1 pound dry spaghetti
2 tablespoons chopped fresh parsley leaves
Freshly grated Parmesan cheese

Heat the oil in a large skillet over medium heat. Add the garlic clove and cook until light golden brown on all sides. Remove the garlic and discard. Add the onions and season with salt to taste.

Cook, stirring occasionally, until the onions are deep golden brown but not burned, 25 to 30 minutes. Add the chopped red pepper and cook 5 minutes longer. Turn off the heat and set aside.

While the onions are cooking, bring a large pot of water to a rolling boil over high heat. Add the tablespoon of salt and the spaghetti. Cook, stirring occasionally, until the pasta is tender but firm, *al dente*, 7 to 10 minutes. Drain; transfer to the skillet with the onions and pepper. Add the parsley and toss well to combine all the ingredients. Serve in preheated individual serving bowls with grated Parmesan.

SPAGHETTI WITH BLACK OLIVE PASTE AND SUN-DRIED TOMATOES

4 TO 6 SERVINGS

This recipe comes from Franco Colombani, owner of the restaurant and inn Albergo del Sole in Lombardy in Italy. Pasta with olive paste has an intensely rich, olivey taste. It is a dish that dates back to ancient Roman times.

3 tablespoons prepared olive paste (see note below)
1 clove garlic, peeled
1 teaspoon small capers, drained
Pinch of hot red pepper flakes
$^1/_2$ cup olive oil
1 tablespoon kosher salt
1 pound dry spaghetti
$^1/_4$ cup chopped Nicoise, Gaeta, or Calamata olives for garnish
2 oil-packed sun-dried tomatoes, sliced into thin strips, for
    garnish
Freshly grated Parmesan cheese

In a food processor fitted with the metal blade or in a blender, combine the olive paste, garlic, capers, and red pepper flakes. Process about 1 minute until the mixture is smooth. Scrape down the sides of the food processor bowl and process 10 seconds longer. With the machine running, slowly pour the olive oil into the processor. Transfer the mixture to a small bowl or container and set aside.

Bring a large pot of water to a rolling boil over high heat. Add the salt and spaghetti. Cook, stirring occasionally, until the pasta is tender but firm, *al dente*, 7 to 10 minutes. Drain; transfer the pasta to preheated individual serving bowls. Stir the olive paste sauce and spoon a few tablespoons over each serving of pasta. Garnish with the chopped olives and sun-dried tomatoes. Serve with Parmesan.

Note: Sold commercially as *olivada*, olive paste is made from ground or finely chopped black or green olives, olive oil, and vinegar, with the optional addition of other flavorings such as lemon juice, herbs, and spices. It is an extremely old Italian preparation for olives, dating back to ancient times, according to the book *A Taste of Ancient Rome* by Ilaria Giacosa (University of Chicago Press, 1993), but olive paste only became available in the United States in recent years. You can buy jars of olive paste in specialty food shops, but I find that prepared olive paste tends to have an overly strong and salty flavor. It is very easy to make your own if you have a food processor or blender. And when you make it at home you can give it just the flavor you like.

To make olive paste, you can use almost any type of olive — oil or brine cured, black or green. I prefer black Gaeta olives from southern Italy, which have a wonderfully delicate flavor and just the right amount of firmness, or oil-cured olives.

Use an olive- or cherry-pitter or small paring knife to remove the pits from the olives. A half-pound of olives makes about 1 cup of pitted olives—enough to make $1/2$ cup olive paste.

Put the pitted olives in a food processor fitted with a steel blade or in a blender and process until they are finely chopped. With the machine running, add $1/4$ cup olive oil, 1 teaspoon red wine vinegar, and 1 teaspoon lemon juice. Continue processing until the mixture is a fine paste. Transfer to a container with a tight-fitting lid and store in the refrigerator until ready to use. It will keep for several months.

SPAGHETTINI WITH FRESH PUMPKIN AND PARMESAN

4 TO 6 SERVINGS

This is a delicious, delicately flavored fall dish from the region around Mantova in Lombardy in northern Italy where the *zucca*, pumpkin squash, is the city's symbol.

$1/3$ cup olive oil
1 clove garlic, pressed or finely minced
1 pound fresh pumpkin or Hubbard squash, peeled, seeds
    removed, and coarsely grated (to yield 3 cups)
1 tablespoon kosher salt, plus extra for seasoning
Freshly ground black pepper
1 pound dry spaghettini
$1/4$ cup chopped fresh parsley leaves
$1/2$ cup freshly grated Parmesan cheese
1 tablespoon, approximately, extra virgin olive oil

Heat the olive oil in a medium-size skillet over medium-high heat. Add the garlic, grated pumpkin, and salt and pepper to taste. As soon as the pumpkin begins to lose its bright orange color and turn yellow, reduce the heat to medium-low and simmer, stirring occasionally, until the pumpkin is tender, about 20 minutes. Turn off the heat and set aside. Reheat before serving.

Bring a large pot of water to a rolling boil over high heat. Add the tablespoon of salt and the spaghettini. Cook, stirring occasionally, until the pasta is tender but firm, *al dente*, 7 to 10 minutes. Drain; transfer the pasta to a large preheated serving bowl. Add the cooked pumpkin, parsley, and Parmesan; toss to combine. Drizzle on the extra virgin olive oil; serve immediately.

BOW TIES WITH WATERCRESS AND TALEGGIO CHEESE

4 SERVINGS

Perfectly ripe taleggio should have a strong aroma—but don't be put off by it; when cooked, it imparts a mild but delicately distinctive taste to the dish.

3 tablespoons olive oil
1 clove garlic, pressed or finely minced
1 bunch fresh watercress, thickest stems discarded, leaves rinsed well, and chopped (to yield 2 cups)
1 tablespoon kosher salt, plus extra for seasoning
1/2 pound dry bow ties
4 ounces taleggio cheese, at room temperature, rind discarded and cut into 1/2-inch cubes
Freshly ground black pepper
Freshly grated Parmesan cheese

Heat the oil in a medium-size skillet over medium-high heat. Add the garlic and watercress. Cook, stirring, until the watercress is wilted and cooked through, about 3 minutes. Turn off the heat and set aside.

Bring a large pot of water to a rolling boil over high heat. Add the tablespoon of salt and the bow ties. Cook, stirring occasionally, until the pasta is tender but firm, *al dente*, 7 to 10 minutes. Drain; immediately transfer to the skillet with the watercress. Turn the heat to medium and add the taleggio and $1/2$ cup of the pasta water. Cook, tossing the pasta with the watercress and cheese until the cheese is completely melted and has created a creamy sauce. Season with salt and freshly ground black pepper. Transfer to preheated individual serving plates; serve with Parmesan.

ROTINI WITH WALNUT SAUCE

4 SERVINGS

Pasta with walnut sauce is a specialty of the Italian region of Liguria. Walnut sauce is wonderful on all types of pasta, but rotini are particularly good because the twisted shape holds the grainy sauce perfectly in its ridges. This is a very rich sauce; a little goes a long way.

$1/4$ cup ($1/2$ stick) unsalted butter
1 tablespoon olive oil
$1/2$ cup ground or finely chopped walnuts
1 cup heavy cream
1 tablespoon kosher salt, plus extra for seasoning
Freshly ground black pepper
$1/2$ pound dry rotini
Freshly grated Parmesan cheese

Place the butter and oil in a medium-size skillet over medium-high heat. When the butter is melted and bubbly, stir in the ground walnuts and add the heavy cream. Season with salt and pepper to taste. Bring the cream to a boil and reduce the heat to medium; simmer until the sauce has thickened, about 5 minutes. Turn off the heat and set aside.

Bring a large pot of water to a rolling boil over high heat. Add the tablespoon of salt and the rotini; cook, stirring occasionally, until the pasta is tender but firm, *al dente*, 7 to 10 minutes. Drain; add to the skillet with the cream and walnut mixture. Reduce the heat to low while tossing the pasta with the sauce until thoroughly coated. Serve immediately.

LIGURIAN-STYLE SPAGHETTI WITH ZUCCHINI, CARROTS, AND CHOPPED FRESH TOMATO

4 TO 6 SERVINGS

This pasta was served as an antipasto at the Hotel Splendido in Portofino, on the Italian Riviera. Because pasta is rarely offered on menus as an antipasto, (it's usally a *primi,* first course) I ordered it just to find out what it was. What I discovered was a surprisingly light, delicious terrine of spaghetti with lots of vegetables and garlic, and wonderful Ligurian olive oil. It can be served as a first course or as a main dish.

4 plum tomatoes, seeded and chopped
1/4 cup plus 1 teaspoon chopped fresh basil leaves
2 tablespoons chopped fresh parsley leaves

⅓ cup plus 2 tablespoons extra virgin olive oil, preferably
   from Liguria such as Ranieri olive oil
2 cloves garlic, pressed or finely chopped
1 small onion, cut in half and thinly sliced
1 medium carrot, peeled and cut into small julienne strips
1 small zucchini, ends discarded and cut into small julienne strips
1 small summer squash, ends discarded and cut into small
   julienne strips
1 tablespoon kosher salt, plus extra for seasoning
1 pound dry spaghetti
Freshly grated Parmesan cheese

In a small mixing bowl, combine the tomatoes with 1 teaspoon of
the basil, 1 tablespoon of the parsley, and 2 tablespoons of the olive
oil; set aside. Heat the remaining ⅓ cup olive oil in a medium-size
skillet over medium heat. Add the garlic, onion, and carrot; season
with salt to taste. Cook, stirring frequently, 5 minutes. Add the
zucchini and summer squash; season with salt to taste and continue cooking 5 minutes longer. Turn off the heat. Stir in the remaining basil and parsley; set aside.

   Meanwhile, bring a large pot of water to a rolling boil over high
heat. Add the tablespoon of salt and the spaghetti. Cook, stirring
frequently, until the pasta is tender but firm, *al dente*, 7 to 10 minutes. Drain the pasta; add it to the skillet with the vegetables. Toss
well to combine. Add salt to taste. Serve in individual preheated
bowls. Top each serving with some of the tomato mixture; serve
with Parmesan.

▦ PENNE WITH ZUCCHINI, SUMMER SQUASH, AND BASIL

4 TO 6 SERVINGS

This is a variation on the classic southern Italian *pasta e zucchine;* the yellow squash makes for a colorful change. Serve with some good grated Parmesan.

$\frac{1}{3}$ cup extra virgin olive oil

2 cloves garlic, pressed or finely minced

3 small zucchini (about 1 pound), ends discarded and thinly sliced into rounds

3 small summer squash (about 1 pound), ends discarded and thinly sliced into rounds

1 tablespoon kosher salt, plus extra for seasoning

1 pound dry penne

$\frac{1}{2}$ cup freshly grated Parmesan cheese

Heat the oil in a medium-size skillet over medium-high heat. Add the garlic, zucchini, and summer squash; season with salt to taste. Cook, stirring, until the zucchini and squash are tender, about 5 minutes. Turn off the heat and set aside.

Bring a large pot of water to a rolling boil over high heat. Add the tablespoon of salt and the penne. Cook, stirring occasionally, until tender but firm, *al dente*, 7 to 10 minutes. Drain; transfer to a large preheated serving bowl. Add the zucchini, squash, and the Parmesan; toss well. Serve immediately.

ANGEL HAIR FRITTATA WITH HERBS AND CHEESES

8 SERVINGS

This pasta pancake makes a great hors d'oeuvre or antipasto dish to serve with drinks before dinner. The pancake should be quite thin and crisp and brown on both sides. I've made this recipe with all types of pasta, and the best is the thinnest angel hair.

6 ounces dry angel hair pasta
1 tablespoon kosher salt
4 large eggs
$\frac{1}{2}$ cup chopped fresh herbs such as parsley, basil, marjoram, chives, and oregano or a mixture of several
8 ounces Italian fontina cheese, rind removed and coarsely grated
$\frac{1}{3}$ cup freshly grated Parmesan cheese, plus extra for serving
2 tablespoons unsalted butter
$\frac{1}{4}$ cup olive oil

Bring a large pot of water to a rolling boil over high heat. Add the angel hair and salt. Cook, stirring occasionally, until the pasta is tender but firm, *al dente*, 5 to 7 minutes. Drain; rinse under cool water.

Break the eggs into a large mixing bowl and beat lightly. Add the cooked pasta, herbs, and cheeses. Using a fork, toss the ingredients until they are thoroughly combined. Because the mixture will be stiff and heavy, it will require a few minutes of stirring to distribute the eggs and cheeses evenly through the pasta.

Heat 1 tablespoon of the butter with 2 tablespoons of the oil in a 10-inch skillet or omelet pan, preferably one with a nonstick surface, over medium heat until the butter is melted and bubbly. Divide the pasta mixture in half (about 3 cups) and spread in an even layer in the bottom of the pan. Reduce the heat to low; cook until the bottom of the frittata is golden brown and holds together when you lift it with a spatula, 15 to 20 minutes. Using two spatulas, one under and one on top, turn the frittata over. Continue cooking until the underside is golden brown, about 10 minutes longer. Transfer to a serving platter. Wipe out the pan and repeat with the remaining butter, oil, and pasta-and-egg mixture. Serve with Parmesan.

CRISPY PASTA AND BROCCOLI PANCAKE

4 SERVINGS

This recipe was inspired by one of my favorite dishes, Chinese pan-fried noodles. You'll turn out a wonderfully crispy-on-the-outside-and-tender-on-the-inside pancake when you use long strands of egg noodle pasta. (Leftover, unsauced pasta works well in this recipe.) I like the taste of broccoli and scallion in the pancake, but you can substitute other vegetables; just make sure that you chop them finely because large pieces of vegetables prevent the pancake from holding together.

8 ounces dry or fresh egg linguine, spaghettini, or fettucine
1 tablespoon kosher salt
$\frac{1}{2}$ cup cooked finely chopped broccoli florets
2 scallions, root ends cut off and discarded, chopped
3 tablespoons olive oil

Bring a large pot of water to a rolling boil. Add the pasta and a tablespoon of salt. Cook, stirring occasionally, until the pasta is tender but firm, *al dente*, about 5 minutes. Drain; allow to stand until cool. Transfer to a large mixing bowl. Add the broccoli and scallions; toss well to combine.

Heat the oil in a 10-inch skillet or omelet pan, preferably one with a nonstick surface, over medium-high heat. When the oil is hot but not smoking, add the pasta and, working quickly with a fork, spread it out in a single even layer. Cook until the underside is golden brown and you can lift the pancake in one piece with a spatula, about 5 minutes. With one spatula under the pancake and one on top, lift and turn the pancake over. Continue cooking until the underside is well browned, about 5 minutes longer. Transfer to a serving plate and serve immediately.

FLAVORED PASTAS

There has always been whole wheat pasta—not only in health food stores but in Italy as well. And for as long as anyone can remember there has been green spinach pasta. But culinary boundaries being what they are—to be crossed and exceeded—when American cooks began experimenting with flavored pasta about a decade ago, the idea of flavoring not only the sauce, but also the pasta, took hold. It wasn't long before pasta shops were rivaling ice cream parlors with their lists of flavors: tomato, mushroom, black pepper, hot pepper, lemon, and herb-flavored pastas were offered, along with many others. Before long, these specialty pastas could be found not only in boutique pasta shops but also in supermarkets. Now they can be prepared at home as easily as plain pasta (see pages 11–12).

Flavored pasta has the advantage of adding some intensity of flavor to a dish—an intensity that you won't get from just a sauce.

All the following recipes call for a particular flavored pasta; you can substitute plain pasta for them.

✳ HERBED LINGUINE WITH SWEET POTATOES AND BUTTERNUT SQUASH

4 SERVINGS

This recipe was inspired by a dish I enjoyed at Wolfgang Puck's restaurant Postrio in San Francisco. If herb- or basil-flavored linguine is not available, use plain unflavored linguine, but add more pesto to the recipe.

$1/3$ cup olive oil
1 clove garlic, pressed or finely minced
$1/2$ pound Hubbard squash or pumpkin, peeled, seeded, and cut into $1/4$-inch dice (about 2 cups)
1 medium-size sweet potato or yam, peeled and cut into $1/4$-inch dice (about 1 cup)
1 tablespoon kosher salt, plus extra for seasoning
$1/2$ pound fresh herb-flavored or plain linguine
1 tablespoon Fresh Pesto Sauce (see page 112)
Freshly grated Parmesan cheese

Heat the oil in a medium-size skillet over medium-high heat. Add the garlic, squash, and sweet potato; season with salt. Cook, stirring occasionally, until the squash is tender and lightly browned, about 20 minutes.

Bring a large pot of water to a rolling boil over high heat. Add the tablespoon of salt and the linguine. Cook, stirring occasionally, until the pasta is tender but firm, *al dente*, about 5 minutes (longer if you are using dry pasta). Drain; transfer to a large preheated serving dish. Add the sweet potato and squash to the pasta with the pesto. Toss well; serve with Parmesan.

HOT RED PEPPER FETTUCINE WITH ROASTED SWEET PEPPER SAUCE

4 SERVINGS

If hot pepper fettucine is not available, use unflavored fettucine and add a pinch of hot red pepper flakes to the sweet peppers.

2 medium-size yellow bell peppers, cut in half lengthwise and
    cores and seeds removed
1 medium-size red bell pepper, cut in half lengthwise and core and
    seeds removed
1/4 cup olive oil
1 clove garlic, pressed or finely minced
1 tablespoon kosher salt, plus extra for seasoning
2 tablespoons hot broth (see pages 121–26)
1/2 pound hot pepper fettucine
2 tablespoons chopped fresh parsley leaves
Freshly grated Parmesan cheese

Preheat the oven broiler. Place the peppers cut side down on an aluminum foil-covered baking sheet; place under the oven broiler on the topmost rack. Broil until the peppers are completely black, about 8 minutes. Remove from the broiler, cover loosely with foil, and allow to stand 10 minutes. Under cold running water, peel the blackened skins from the peppers. Pat dry with paper towels; slice the peppers lengthwise into thin strips. You should have about 2 cups sliced peppers.

Heat the oil in a medium-size skillet over medium heat. Add the garlic and roasted peppers; season with salt. Cook, stirring, until the peppers are heated through, about 3 minutes. Add the broth and cook until the pepper sauce has thickened.

Meanwhile, bring a large pot of water to a rolling boil over high heat. Add the tablespoon of salt and the fettucine. Cook, stirring occasionally, until tender but firm, *al dente*, about 5 minutes. (If you are using dry fettucine, cook the pasta longer, 7 to 10 minutes.) Drain; transfer to a large preheated serving bowl. Add the peppers and the parsley; toss well. Serve with Parmesan.

SPINACH FETTUCINE WITH FRESH TOMATO SAUCE AND CREAMY RICOTTA

4 SERVINGS

Incredibly simple to prepare, this is a stunning dish to behold: the green, red, and white colors of the Italian flag are strikingly composed on each plate. You can use either fresh or dried pasta, but green spinach-flavored pasta is essential. If you don't have the time to prepare fresh tomato sauce, use a good store-bought marinara.

1 cup Fresh Tomato Sauce (see page 86)
$1/2$ cup whole-milk ricotta cheese
1 tablespoon mascarpone cheese
$1/2$ pound spinach fettucine or other spinach pasta
1 tablespoon kosher salt
Freshly grated Parmesan cheese

In a small saucepan, heat the tomato sauce over medium heat until hot and bubbling. In a small bowl, combine the ricotta and mascarpone; mix well with a wire whisk or fork.

Bring a large pot of water to a rolling boil over high heat. Add the fettucine and salt. Cook, stirring occasionally, until tender but firm, *al dente*, 5 minutes. (If you are using dry pasta, cook the pasta longer, 7 to 10 minutes.) Drain; transfer to preheated individual serving bowls. Top each serving of pasta with $1/4$ cup of tomato sauce and a generous spoonful of the ricotta mixture. Serve with Parmesan.

SPINACH FETTUCINE WITH SWEET PEAS AND FRESH HERBS

4 SERVINGS

Peas have been a staple of Italian cuisine since the time of ancient Rome. But sweet peas have been grown in Italy only since the sixteenth century after Catherine d'Medici sent them from France. The combination of peas and mint has become a classic Italian preparation. This variation calls for a mixture of mint, basil, and parsley. Spinach pasta makes for a very green dish. It's also wonderful with egg fettucine.

$1/4$ cup ($1/2$ stick) unsalted butter
1 large clove garlic, pressed or finely minced
1 cup fresh sweet peas or defrosted frozen peas
1 tablespoon chopped fresh mint leaves
1 tablespoon chopped fresh parsley leaves
1 tablespoon chopped fresh basil leaves
1 tablespoon kosher salt, plus extra for seasoning
$1/2$ pound dry or fresh spinach fettucine
$1/4$ cup freshly grated Parmesan cheese, plus extra for serving

In a large skillet, heat the butter with the garlic over medium heat until the butter is bubbling. Add the peas; cook until the peas are heated through, 2 to 3 minutes. Add the mint, parsley, and basil; season with salt to taste. Turn off the heat and set aside.

Meanwhile, bring a large pot of water to a rolling boil over high heat. Add the tablespoon of salt and the fettucine. Cook, stirring occasionally, until the pasta is tender but firm, *al dente*, about 5 minutes. (If using dry pasta, cook 7 to 10 minutes.) Drain; transfer to the skillet with the peas. Add the Parmesan; toss well. Season with salt to taste. Serve with more Parmesan.

Many varieties of mint—both cultivated and wild—grow in Italy and are used in cooking. Wild mint, called *mentuccia*, has a smaller leaf and a much milder flavor and aroma than the cultivated peppermint we know. Another type of mint, *nepitella*, which tastes like a cross between marjoram and mint, is typically used in the cooking of Tuscany and in Lazio, the region around Rome.

 # WHOLE WHEAT PASTA WITH POTATOES, CABBAGE, AND FONTINA

4 SERVINGS

This dish, called *pizzoccheri*, is a meal in itself. It comes from the Valtellina area of northern Italy and is traditionally baked in the oven, but I have found it can be prepared on top of the stove with great results.

$^1\!/_3$ cup olive oil

$^1\!/_3$ cup finely chopped onion

1 clove garlic, pressed or finely minced

1 medium-size carrot, cut into matchstick strips (about 1 cup)

1 medium-size boiling potato, preferably Yukon Gold, peeled
   and cut into julienne strips (about 1 cup)

1 cup finely shredded Savoy cabbage

6 fresh sage leaves

4 ounces Italian fontina cheese, at room temperature,
   rind removed and cut into 1-inch cubes

$^1\!/_2$ pound dry whole wheat linguine or fettucine

1 tablespoon kosher salt, plus extra for seasoning

Freshly ground black pepper

Freshly grated Parmesan cheese

Heat the oil in a large skillet over medium heat. Add the onion and garlic; cook until the onion begins to soften, 2 to 3 minutes. Add the carrot and potato; continue cooking, stirring occasionally, until the vegetables are tender when pierced with a sharp knife, about 5 minutes longer. Add the cabbage and sage leaves. Cook, stirring, until the cabbage is cooked through, about 5 minutes longer. Turn off the heat and set aside.

Bring a large pot of water to a rolling boil over high heat. Add the whole wheat pasta and the tablespoon of salt. Cook, stirring occasionally, until the pasta is tender but firm, *al dente*, 8 to 10 minutes. Drain; transfer the pasta to the skillet with the cabbage and potato mixture. Add the fontina and $^1\!/_4$ cup of pasta water; cook over medium-low heat until the cheese is melted and combined with the vegetables. Season with salt and pepper to taste. Serve with Parmesan.

PASTA WITH ROASTED VEGETABLE SAUCES

Oven-roasted vegetables have a wonderfully intense flavor that can't be matched by cooking them any other way. In high oven heat, the water in the vegetables cooks away quickly, leaving the natural sugars caramelized and the vegetables deliciously browned and tasty. Roasted vegetable sauces are among the most flavorful and also among the easiest to prepare. The results will give you rave notices.

LINGUINE WITH ROASTED PLUM TOMATOES AND FRESH HERBS

6 SERVINGS

Roasted tomatoes have an unusually intense, luscious taste that you won't get from cooking on top of the stove. You don't have to peel the tomatoes for this dish, just remove the seeds and cores. Serve this pasta with the best Parmesan, Parmigiano-Reggiano; it makes a delicious difference.

$^1\!/_3$ cup plus 2 tablespoons olive oil

3 pounds plum tomatoes, seeded and cored and cut into
    1-inch pieces

3 tablespoons chopped fresh parsley leaves

2 tablespoons chopped fresh oregano or marjoram leaves

1 tablespoon chopped fresh basil leaves

2 cloves garlic, pressed or finely minced

1 tablespoon kosher salt, plus extra for seasoning

1 pound dry linguine

Freshly grated Parmigiano-Reggiano cheese

Preheat the oven to 450°F. Pour ⅓ cup of the oil into a large roasting pan and add the tomatoes, herbs, and garlic. Stir well to coat the tomatoes with the oil; spread them in an even layer in the pan, and sprinkle with salt to taste. Roast in the oven, stirring every 10 minutes, on the topmost rack until the tomatoes are beginning to turn brown, 20 to 25 minutes. Remove from the oven and set aside.

While the tomatoes are roasting, bring a large pot of water to a rolling boil over high heat. Add the tablespoon of salt and the linguine. Cook, until the linguine is tender but firm, *al dente*, 7 to 10 minutes. Drain; transfer to a large preheated serving bowl. Pour the roasted tomatoes over the pasta. Add the remaining olive oil; toss well. Serve with the Parmigiano-Reggiano.

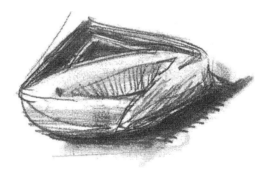

▓ ORECCHIETTE WITH SPICY ROASTED CAULIFLOWER, TOMATOES, AND ONIONS

4 SERVINGS

This dish was inspired by cauliflower and tomatoes *al arrabbiata*, a spicy southern Italian recipe. The spicy taste comes from red pepper flakes. If your tastes run to the milder side, you can omit the pepper.

1 small head cauliflower (about 1 ½ pounds), cut into
    bite-size florets
1 large onion, coarsely chopped (to yield 2 cups)
1 ½ pounds fresh plum tomatoes, seeded and coarsely
    chopped (to yield about 3 cups)
½ cup olive oil
½ teaspoon hot red pepper flakes
1 tablespoon kosher salt, plus extra for seasoning
½ pound dry orecchiette
2 tablespoons chopped fresh parsley leaves
Freshly grated Parmesan cheese

Preheat the oven to 450°F. Combine the cauliflower, onion, and tomatoes in a large roasting pan. Add the olive oil, red pepper flakes, and salt to taste. Stir to combine; spread the vegetables in the pan in an even layer. Place the pan on the topmost rack in the oven; roast, stirring occasionally to prevent the vegetables from sticking, until the cauliflower is golden brown, 25 to 30 minutes. Remove from the oven and set aside.

While the vegetables are roasting, bring a large pot of water to a rolling boil over high heat. Add the tablespoon of salt and the orecchiette. Cook, stirring occasionally, until the pasta is tender but firm, *al dente*, about 10 minutes. Drain; transfer to a large pre-heated serving bowl. Add the roasted cauliflower and tomatoes; toss well. Garnish with the parsley. Serve with Parmesan.

❖ RIGATONI WITH ROASTED EGGPLANT, SUN-DRIED TOMATOES, AND GOAT CHEESE

4 SERVINGS

This is a flavorful dish that you can serve hot or cold. The bulky shape of the rigatoni complements the chunky sauce. You can use one of the many American or French goat cheeses available, but use only a fresh, not aged, unflavored cheese.

1 medium-size eggplant (about 1 1/2 pounds), stem end discarded
   and cut into 1-inch cubes
1 tablespoon kosher salt, plus extra for sprinkling on eggplant
1/3 cup olive oil
1 cup loosely packed oil-packed sun-dried tomatoes, drained
2 tablespoons oil from the sun-dried tomatoes
3 tablespoons chopped fresh parsley leaves
1/2 pound dry rigatoni
2 ounces fresh unflavored goat cheese, crumbled
Freshly grated Parmesan cheese

Preheat the oven to 450°F. Place the eggplant cubes in a colander and sprinkle lightly with salt. Allow eggplant to stand and drain about 30 minutes. Pour the olive oil into a baking dish; add the eggplant and toss well to combine. Place the roasting pan in the oven and roast, stirring occasionally, until the eggplant is well browned, about 20 minutes.

Meanwhile, put the sun-dried tomatoes in a food processor fitted with the steel blade and process until coarsely chopped, 10 to 15 seconds; be careful not to overprocess the tomatoes into a paste. Add the sun-dried tomato oil and parsley; turn the machine on and off to combine. Set aside.

Meanwhile, bring a large pot of water to a rolling boil over high heat. Add the tablespoon of salt and the rigatoni. Cook, stirring frequently, until the pasta is tender but firm, *al dente*, 7 to 10 minutes. Drain; transfer to a preheated serving dish. Add the roasted eggplant and sun-dried tomatoes to the pasta; toss well. Sprinkle the crumbled goat cheese over the top; serve with Parmesan.

Goat cheese is called *caprino* in Italian, and many different versions are produced throughout Italy. In general, goat cheese has a crumbly, soft texture and a pungent, piercing flavor and salty taste. It does not melt particularly well because it is low in butterfat, but it is just as delicious hot and cooked as it is cold.

PENNE WITH ROASTED EGGPLANT, TOMATOES, AND ONIONS

4 TO 6 SERVINGS

This is my daughter's Annie's favorite. Use fresh herbs if possible. You can substitute fresh oregano or basil for the marjoram.

1 large eggplant (about 1½ pounds), stem end cut off and
    discarded and cut into 1-inch cubes
1 tablespoon kosher salt, plus extra for sprinkling on eggplant
    and seasoning
½ cup olive oil
2 pounds plum tomatoes, seeded and coarsely chopped
1 large onion, peeled and coarsely chopped
2 cloves garlic, pressed or finely minced
2 tablespoons chopped fresh marjoram, oregano, or basil leaves
1 pound dry penne
2 tablespoons chopped fresh parsley leaves
2 tablespoons extra virgin olive oil
Freshly grated pecorino romano cheese

Preheat the oven to 450°F. Place the cubed eggplant in a colander
and sprinkle lightly with salt; toss. Allow eggplant to drain, at least
30 minutes. Pour the oil into a large roasting pan. Add the eggplant, tomatoes, onion, garlic, and marjoram. Season with salt to
taste; stir well to coat the vegetables with oil. Spread the vegetables in an even layer in the pan. Place the roasting pan in the oven
on the topmost rack; roast, stirring occasionally, until the eggplant
and onions are lightly browned, 25 to 30 minutes.

　　While the vegetables are roasting, bring a large pot of water to a
rolling boil over high heat. Add the tablespoon of salt and the
penne. Cook, stirring occasionally, until the pasta is tender but
firm, *al dente*, 7 to 10 minutes. Drain; immediately add the pasta to
the roasting pan with the vegetables. Add the parsley and extra
virgin olive oil; toss well. Transfer to a large preheated serving
dish. Serve with grated pecorino romano cheese.

PENNE WITH ROASTED FENNEL AND ONIONS

4 SERVINGS

Intensely flavorful, this recipe gives you lots of fennel and sweet onion taste.

2 fennel bulbs (about 2 pounds total), tall stalks and leaves discarded, bulb cut in half lengthwise and cut crosswise into ¼-inch-thick slices
1 large Spanish onion or 2 medium-size yellow onions, peeled, cut in half, and sliced ¼-inch thick
1 large clove garlic, pressed or finely minced
½ cup olive oil
1 tablespoon kosher salt, plus extra for seasoning
½ pound dry penne
2 tablespoons chopped fresh parsley leaves
Freshly grated Parmesan cheese

Preheat the oven to 450°F. Combine the fennel, onion, garlic, and oil in a large roasting pan. Season with salt to taste; toss the mixture to coat the fennel and onion with the oil. Spread the vegetable mixture in an even layer in the pan. Roast on the topmost rack in the oven, stirring occasionally, until the fennel and onions are just beginning to turn brown, 20 to 25 minutes. Be careful not to overcook; the fennel and onion will quicky go from brown to burned.

While the vegetables are roasting, bring a large pot of water to a rolling boil over high heat. Add the tablespoon of salt and the penne. Cook, stirring occasionally, until the pasta is tender but firm, *al dente*, 7 to 10 minutes. Drain; transfer to a large preheated serving bowl. Add the roasted fennel and onion and the parsley; toss well. Serve with grated Parmesan.

PENNE WITH ROASTED ELEPHANT GARLIC, ROSEMARY, AND GOAT CHEESE

4 SERVINGS

Elephant garlic is milder than ordinary garlic but extremely flavorful when roasted. I've always enjoyed it spread on bread or crostini, but I was delighted to find that it's equally good when blended with goat cheese and tossed with pasta. Before roasting the garlic, line your roasting pan with aluminum foil because the garlic will burn it irreparably, as I discovered the first time I roasted garlic. This recipe calls for only a modest amount of garlic, but feel free to add more if you're so inclined.

3 large cloves elephant garlic
$1/4$ cup plus 2 tablespoons olive oil
1 tablespoon kosher salt, plus extra for seasoning
2 tablespoons water
$1/2$ pound dry penne
5 sprigs fresh rosemary
3 ounces fresh unflavored goat cheese (local American varieties work very well in this dish), crumbled

Preheat the oven to 500°F. Line a small heat-resistant pan with aluminum foil. Place the garlic cloves in the pan with 2 tablespoons of the oil. Coat the cloves with the oil; sprinkle lightly with salt. Add the water and cover tightly with more foil. Place in the oven and roast 45 minutes. Uncover and roast until the garlic is completely tender (it should be quite soft), about 10 minutes longer. Remove from the oven; set aside to cool slightly. When you can handle the cloves, pull the skins, which will be stiff, from the garlic; cut the cloves into 3 or 4 pieces. Set aside.

Bring a large pot of water to a rolling boil over high heat. Add the tablespoon of salt and the penne. Cook, stirring occasionally, until the pasta is tender but firm, *al dente*, 7 to 10 minutes. Drain.

Meanwhile, heat the remaining ¼ cup of oil in a medium-size skillet over medium heat. Add a sprig of the rosemary and cook about 2 minutes to flavor the oil. Remove the rosemary; lower the heat to medium-low and add the roasted garlic, pasta, and goat cheese. Toss well until the cheese is melted and creamy. Serve immediately in individual serving bowls. Garnish with sprigs of fresh rosemary.

In ancient times, rosemary was used for dozens of medicinal and mythological purposes. A beautiful bush with leaves that resemble those of a pine tree, rosemary is typically used in Italian cooking as a flavoring for roasted meat and the roasted potatoes that accompany it. Although fresh rosemary has a pungent, perfumy aroma, the fragrance mellows considerably when cooked. Fresh rosemary is durable and keeps for up to a week in the refrigerator.

RIGATONI WITH ROASTED SWEET ONIONS AND BALSAMIC VINEGAR

4 TO 6 SERVINGS

The sweetness of the onions is offset by the delicate tartness of the balsamic vinegar. If Vidalia onions aren't in season, use Spanish or Bermuda onions.

2 pounds Vidalia or other sweet onions, peeled and cut into
 $1/2$-inch wedges
$1/4$ cup olive oil
1 tablespoon kosher salt, plus extra for seasoning
1 pound dry rigatoni
1 tablespoon balsamic vinegar (see page 26), or more to taste
2 tablespoons chopped fresh parsley leaves
Freshly grated Parmesan cheese

Preheat the oven to 450°F. Place the onion wedges in a roasting pan large enough to accommodate them in a single layer. Pour the olive oil over the onions; turn them around to make sure that they are completely coated with the oil. Lightly sprinkle the onions with salt; place on topmost rack in the oven. Roast until the edges are well browned but not burned, 20 to 25 minutes.

While the onions are roasting, bring a large pot of water to a rolling boil over high heat. Add the tablespoon of salt and the rigatoni. Cook, stirring occasionally, until the pasta is tender but firm, *al dente*, 7 to 10 minutes. Drain; transfer to a large preheated serving bowl. Pour the roasted onions over the pasta. Add the balsamic vinegar and parsley; toss well. Season with more salt to taste. Serve with Parmesan.

BOW TIES WITH GARLICKY SPINACH AND ROASTED FIGS

4 SERVINGS

This dish was inspired by the traditional southern Italian preparation for spinach, which calls for plump golden raisins. Deliciously ripe figs, roasted in the oven, are a wonderful substitute for the sweetness of the raisins.

Look for figs that are ripe, but not past their prime; they should be firm, but yield slightly to the touch. Be careful not to overcook the figs. If the figs are large, figure one whole fig per serving; for smaller figs, count $1\frac{1}{2}$ to 2 per serving.

4 large ripe figs or 6 smaller ones, cut in half lengthwise
$\frac{1}{3}$ cup olive oil
1 tablespoon kosher salt
$\frac{1}{2}$ pound dry bow ties
2 cloves garlic, pressed or finely minced
10 ounces fresh spinach, stems removed, rinsed well in several
    changes of cold water, dried and coarsely chopped

Preheat the oven to 500°F. Line a small roasting pan with aluminum foil; place the figs on the foil, cut side up, and lightly brush them with 1 to 2 tablespoons of the oil. Roast in the oven until tender and just beginning to brown, 5 to 6 minutes. Remove from the oven; cover lightly with foil to keep warm and set aside.

Bring a large pot of water to a rolling boil over high heat. Add the salt and the bow ties. Cook, stirring occasionally, until the pasta is tender but firm, *al dente*, 7 to 10 minutes.

While the pasta is cooking, heat the remaining oil in a medium-size skillet over medium-high heat. Add the garlic and spinach. Cook, stirring, until the spinach is tender, about 5 minutes. Drain the pasta; add to the skillet with the spinach and toss well to combine. Transfer to preheated individual serving bowls. Arrange 2 to 3 halves of roasted figs over each serving. Serve immediately.

ABOUT FIGS

The fig is a fruit that is native to the Mediterranean and thrived in ancient Roman times. Many of the Roman writers talked about figs, their cultivation, their culinary qualities, and the myths surrounding them. Pliny wrote about the particular fig tree where Rome's founders, Romulus and Remus, were found suckling the milk from a she-wolf. The season for enjoying figs is late summer and early autumn. They are extremely perishable once they are ripe and are usually harvested under-ripe and should be allowed to fully ripen before they are eaten. In Italy, figs are eaten both as fruit for dessert and as a first course with prosciutto. Because they are so perishable, figs are often preserved—dried or in a sweet syrup.

❋ BOW TIES WITH ROASTED ZUCCHINI HALF-MOONS AND GARLIC

4 SERVINGS

This simple recipe can be prepared in the oven with little attention required from the cook. Try to time the zucchini so that it's ready just when the pasta is *al dente*; it's best if it doesn't stand too long.

2 pounds small zucchini, ends discarded, cut in half lengthwise, and sliced crosswise into $1/2$-inch-thick slices
1 tablespoon kosher salt, plus extra for sprinkling on zucchini
$1/4$ cup olive oil
1 large clove garlic, pressed or finely minced
$1/2$ pound dry bow ties
2 tablespoons chopped fresh basil leaves
$1/4$ cup freshly grated Parmigiano-Reggiano cheese

Preheat the oven to 450°F. Place the zucchini in a colander; sprinkle lightly with salt and allow to stand and drain, at least 30 minutes. Put the zucchini in a medium-size roasting pan. Add the oil and garlic; toss well to coat the zucchini with the oil. Place in the oven on the topmost rack; roast until the zucchini pieces are golden brown, 25 to 30 minutes.

While the zucchini is roasting, bring a large pot of water to a rolling boil over high heat. Add the tablespoon of salt and the bow ties. Cook, stirring occasionally, until the pasta is tender but firm, *al dente*, 7 to 10 minutes. Drain; transfer to a large preheated serving bowl. Add the roasted zucchini, basil, and cheese; toss well. Serve immediately.

PENNE WITH ROASTED RED PEPPERS, SPINACH, AND GARLIC

4 SERVINGS

The peppers in this dish are roasted with their skins on, which I think adds even more delicious sweet flavor. You can use a mix of pepper colors in this recipe, but I like the contrast of the red peppers and bright green spinach.

2 medium-size red bell peppers, cored, seeded, and sliced
  lengthwise into 1-inch-wide strips
$1/4$ cup olive oil
1 clove garlic, pressed or finely minced
1 tablespoon kosher salt, plus extra for seasoning
$1/2$ pound dry penne
1 cup coarsely chopped fresh spinach leaves with stems
  removed and rinsed well in several changes of cold water
Freshly grated Parmesan cheese

Preheat the oven to 500°F. Place the pepper pieces, skin side down, in a heat-proof baking pan large enough to hold them in a single layer. Pour the olive oil over the peppers and add the garlic. Sprinkle with salt; place on topmost rack in the oven. Roast until the peppers are beginning to brown but are not burned, 15 to 20 minutes. Remove from the oven; set aside.

Meanwhile, bring a large pot of water to a rolling boil over high heat. Add the tablespoon of salt and the penne. Cook, stirring occasionally, until the pasta is tender but still firm, *al dente*, about 7 minutes. Add the chopped spinach and cook 1 minute. Drain; transfer to a large preheated serving bowl. Add the roasted peppers, and salt to taste. Toss; serve with Parmesan.

PASTA WITH TOMATO SAUCES

It is hard to imagine pasta without tomato sauce. More than any other ingredient, tomatoes characterize what a pasta sauce is for most people. But pasta was in Italy long before tomatoes. Tomatoes didn't become part of Italian cuisine until after the discovery of the New World. And even after they arrived in the late sixteenth century and were named *pomodoro*, golden apple, tomatoes were spurned by farmers and cooks alike, and then accepted only gradually.

Sun-dried tomatoes, with their intense tomato taste, are a staple of southern Italian cooking from Calabria and Sicily, where most of the tomatoes are grown in Italy, as well as from the northern region of Liguria. In the fall, when the bulk of tomatoes is harvested, part of the crop is set aside to be dried rather than canned or simmered into sauce. In the drying process, the pear-shaped tomatoes are split and salted and left in the hot sun to dry. When fully dehydrated, they are packed into bags and sold dry or preserved in jars.

If you grow your own tomatoes or have access to an abundant crop, you can make your own dried tomatoes in a standard oven, set at a very low temperature (200°F) for several hours. Before drying, cut the tomatoes in half lengthwise, remove the seeds, sprinkle lightly with kosher salt, and set the tomato halves onto racks rather than sheets so that they dry evenly. You also can use an electric dehydrator, which comes with instructions for preparing tomatoes. You should figure 12 to 16 hours in a standard oven to fully dry the tomatoes. Pack the dried tomatoes into plastic bags

Tomatoes found a place first in Southern Italian cooking because they grew so well in the warm, dry regions of Campania, Abruzzo, and Reggio-Calabria. The earliest recipes for pasta sauce from that area show that tomatoes were usually made into a ragù with meat. In the ninteenth century, tomatoes were cultivated for large-scale processing—making them available beyond the southern regions—and fully incorporated into the regional cuisines throughout Italy.

Tomato sauce can be simple and uncomplicated, prepared only with fresh tomatoes and seasoned with olive oil and garlic; or it

and store in a cool, dark place. Dried tomatoes keep for months.

Whether you make your own dried tomatoes or buy already-dried tomatoes, before you can use them in recipes they must be reconstituted in boiling water. The tomatoes can then be packed in olive oil and stored in the refrigerator.

Bring a small saucepan of water to boil over high heat. Add the dried tomatoes and cook for 5 minutes. Drain the tomatoes. Using a jar or a container with a tight-fitting lid, layer the tomatoes into the jar with whole, peeled cloves of garlic and a sprinkling of dried herbs such as basil and oregano. When all the tomatoes are in the jar, add enough pure olive oil to cover. Press down on the tomatoes to eliminate any air pockets. Tomatoes packed in oil keep in the refrigerator for months and are ready for eating or cooking. Some sun-dried tomatoes turn dark with time. This is okay. It means the tomatoes were not treated with sulfur, which prevents oxidation. It won't affect the taste or texture. Sun-dried tomatoes have a strong, piquant flavor and are often salty; use them sparingly.

can be more elaborate—flavored with vegetables and herbs and highly seasoned. Following are my favorite tomato sauce recipes, beginning with the best and simplest, Fresh Tomato Sauce and several variations for it. This sauce is delicious enough to be served on its own, or it can be combined with other ingredients and transformed into a variety of sauces.

As you will see, for most tomato-based sauces I prefer to use fresh tomatoes that have been peeled and seeded. Even when they are not at their summertime best, small plum tomatoes lend a fresh taste to a dish that can't be duplicated with canned tomatoes. In those recipes calling for canned tomatoes, I like to use chopped or "ground peeled" tomatoes from the can. They lend a nice texture to a dish and are more convenient to use than whole tomatoes, which need to be seeded and drained before they can be added to the pot. In addition to canned tomatoes, tomato concentrate and sun-dried tomatoes can be added to pasta sauces and provide a wonderful intensity of tomato flavor.

Traditionally in Italy, tomato sauces are served with spaghetti or other long strands of pasta. I recommend a pasta for each recipe, but feel free to substitute whatever you might have on hand.

▨ SPAGHETTI WITH FRESH TOMATO SAUCE

6 SERVINGS

The most universal pasta sauce in all Italy, and anywhere else pasta is eaten, is tomato sauce. Sometimes called marinara sauce, the best tomato sauce is made with fresh, ripe—the riper the tomatoes, the more flavorful and rich-tasting the sauce—what we call plum tomatoes and Italians call *pomodori di San Marzano*. These have a high flesh-to-core ratio, which makes a thick, not watery sauce. Plum tomatoes also have a slightly thicker skin compared with other eating tomatoes, making them firmer and easier to peel. If you only have large eating tomatoes, you can make a pasta sauce with them, but the sauce may require more cooking to eliminate excess watery liquid.

As this recipe shows, a fresh tomato sauce needs very little in the way of ingredients for good flavor, but you can add more vegetables or seasonings to your taste. Use a wide, flat-bottomed sauce pan for best results. It helps the watery liquid in the tomatoes to cook away quickly without overcooking the tomatoes.

3 pounds ripe plum tomatoes
$1/4$ cup pure olive oil
1 large clove garlic, pressed or finely minced
1 tablespoon kosher salt, plus extra for seasoning
1 pound dry spaghetti
$1/4$ cup coarsely chopped fresh basil leaves or 2 tablespoons
    fresh chopped parsley leaves, if basil is not available
Freshly grated Parmesan cheese

Peel the tomatoes. Bring 2 quarts water to a boil in a large saucepan on top of the stove. Place the tomatoes in the boiling water. Cook exactly 1 minute. Drain in a colander and allow to cool slightly. Use a sharp paring knife to cut away the stem end of the tomato and peel off the skin. The skin should slip off easily; if it does not, place the tomato back into the boiling water for 30 seconds longer. Cut around the inside core with the knife, and gently squeeze the core and seeds out. Hold the tomato under cold water to flush out any remaining seeds. Coarsely chop the tomatoes.

Heat the oil in a large skillet over medium-high heat. Add the garlic; stir and cook 1 minute, making sure it doesn't brown. Add the tomatoes; stir to combine with the oil and garlic. Liberally season with salt to taste. Reduce the heat to medium; cook, stirring occasionally, until the sauce is thick and the watery liquid in the tomatoes has cooked away, about 20 minutes. You should be able to see some chunks of tomatoes in the sauce. When the sauce has finished cooking, turn off the heat. Taste and add more salt if necessary. Stir in the basil.

Bring a large pot of water to a rolling boil over high heat. Add the tablespoon of salt and the spaghetti. Cook, stirring occasionally, until the pasta is tender but firm, *al dente*, 7 to 10 minutes. Drain; transfer to a large serving bowl. Pour the tomato sauce over the pasta. Serve with Parmesan.

Note: If you like an even-textured, not chunky sauce, prepare this sauce with unpeeled tomatoes: before cooking, remove the cores and seeds from the tomatoes; after cooking, put the sauce through a food mill to extract the skins. Return the sauce to the pan and continue cooking until thick.

Fresh Tomato Sauce/Winter Variation

In the winter when plum tomatoes are not at their best, you can improve this sauce by adding some canned plum tomatoes to the sauce. Reduce the amount of fresh tomatoes to 2 pounds. Follow the directions above and add 1 cup chopped canned plum tomatoes after the tomatoes have been cooking for about 15 minutes. Cook about 5 minutes longer and proceed with the recipe.

Tip: If you want to peel only 2 or 3 tomatoes, heat 3 cups of water in a microwave-safe bowl until boiling, 3 to 4 minutes. Remove from the oven. Drop the tomatoes into the water and let stand 1 minute. Drain; peel as directed above.

ROTINI WITH SUN-DRIED TOMATOES AND SWEET PEAS

6 SERVINGS

Very little cooking is called for in this recipe, making it a wonderful hot-weather dish. If the varieties of fresh peas are not available, you can substitute one kind for another or use frozen baby peas, which should be defrosted but not cooked before adding them to the recipe. If you grow your own sweet peas, try sautéing the greens and serving them as a garnish on this dish.

$\frac{1}{3}$ pound sugar snap peas, stems and veins removed
   (yield 2 cups)
$\frac{1}{3}$ pound snow peas (yield 2 cups)
$\frac{1}{3}$ cup shelled fresh sweet peas
1 cup oil-packed sun-dried tomato halves, drained and
   finely chopped (to yield $\frac{1}{4}$ cup)
$\frac{1}{4}$ cup extra virgin olive oil
1 tablespoon kosher salt
1 pound dry rotini, fusilli, or other squiggly pasta
2 tablespoons chopped fresh parsley leaves
Freshly grated Parmesan cheese

Bring a 2-quart saucepan of water to boil. Drop all the peas into the boiling water and cook exactly 3 minutes. Drain; rinse under cold water to stop the cooking and transfer to a large serving bowl.

Combine the sun-dried tomatoes and olive oil in a small mixing bowl; stir well to combine. Set aside.

Bring a large pot of water to a rolling boil over high heat. Add the salt and rotini. Cook, stirring occasionally, until the pasta is tender but firm, *al dente*, 7 to 10 minutes. Drain; transfer to the serving bowl with the peas. Pour the sun-dried tomato and olive oil mixture over the pasta. Add the parsley; toss well to combine. Serve with Parmesan.

PENNE WITH TOMATO SAUCE AND THREE CHEESES

6 SERVINGS

A simple tomato sauce is made heavenly and incredibly creamy with the addition of fontina, mascarpone, and Parmesan cheeses. I like to serve this dish to large gatherings of friends—it can easily be doubled and holds up to buffet-style serving.

1 tablespoon kosher salt

1 pound dry penne

1 cup Fresh Tomato Sauce (see page 86) or other tomato sauce

4 ounces Italian fontina cheese, at room temperature, rind removed and cut into small cubes

2 tablespoons mascarpone cheese

1/4 cup freshly grated Parmesan cheese, plus extra for serving

1/4 cup chopped fresh basil leaves

Bring a large pot of water to a rolling boil over high heat. Add the salt and penne. Cook, stirring occasionally, until the pasta is tender but firm, *al dente*, 7 to 10 minutes. Drain.

While the pasta is cooking, heat the tomato sauce over medium-low heat in a heavy 4-quart saucepan or casserole from which you can serve the pasta. Add the drained pasta, cheeses, and basil; reduce the heat to low. Stir until the cheeses are melted and the sauce is creamy. Serve with additional Parmesan.

SPAGHETTINI WITH UNCOOKED FRESH TOMATOES, ARUGULA, AND PARMESAN

6 SERVINGS

This fresh-tasting, summery pasta dish is so easy to prepare because all you have to cook is the pasta. The heat from the cooked spaghetti is enough to wilt the arugula and warm the tomatoes perfectly.

6 plum tomatoes (1 pound), seeded and coarsely chopped
1/4 cup extra virgin olive oil
2 bunches fresh arugula, rinsed in several changes of cold water, thickest stems discarded, and leaves coarsely chopped (to yield about 4 cups)
1 tablespoon kosher salt, plus extra for seasoning
1 three-ounce piece Parmigiano-Reggiano or Grana Parmesan cheese
1 pound dry spaghettini
Freshly ground black pepper
Freshly grated Parmesan cheese

Combine the tomatoes, olive oil, and arugula leaves in a large serving bowl. Season with salt to taste. Use a vegetable peeler to shave the cheese into paper-thin shards. Add to the bowl with the tomatoes and arugula; toss well to combine.

Bring a large pot of water to a rolling boil over high heat. Add the tablespoon of salt and the pasta. Cook, stirring occasionally, until the pasta is tender but firm, *al dente*, 7 to 10 minutes. Drain; add to the serving bowl with the tomatoes, oil, arugula, and Parmesan. Toss well; season with more salt and black pepper to taste. Serve with grated Parmesan.

✳ FUSILLI WITH RAW TOMATO SAUCE, BASIL, AND SWEET ONION

6 SERVINGS

On a hot summer night in Milan, my husband and I wandered into the restaurant Don Lisander, an informal place with straightforward food. But as unassuming as the restaurant was, I found this unusual tomato sauce to be exceptional. The maitre d' informed me that the secret behind the sauce was salting the tomatoes and letting them drain for a good hour or more. The salt pulls all the watery liquid from the tomatoes, leaving just the pulp and fresh tomato taste. Serve the sauce at room temperature on hot pasta with an extra drizzle of good fruity olive oil.

1 small sweet yellow onion, cut into quarters
2 pounds ripe plum tomatoes, cored and seeded
1 cup firmly packed fresh basil leaves
2 tablespoons kosher salt
$\frac{1}{2}$ cup extra virgin olive oil, plus more to taste

1 pound dry fusilli, rotini, or other squiggly pasta
Fresh basil leaves for garnish
Freshly grated Parmesan cheese

If you are using a food processor, put the metal blade in place, cover, and turn on the machine. Drop the onion pieces through the feed tube to finely chop. Turn off the machine. Place all the tomatoes and basil in the food processor with the onion; pulse or process until the tomatoes are finely chopped but not puréed. (Or finely chop the tomatoes, onion, and basil by hand.) Place the tomato mixture in a large wire mesh strainer or colander. Sprinkle with 1 tablespoon of the salt; allow to stand at least an hour, stirring occasionally, to drain as much liquid from the tomatoes as possible. Transfer the tomato-and-onion mixture to a small mixing bowl (you should have about 2 cups). Add the oil; stir and set aside.

Bring a large pot of water to a rolling boil over high heat. Add the remaining salt and the fusilli. Cook, stirring occasionally, until the pasta is tender but firm, *al dente*, 7 to 10 minutes. Drain well; transfer the pasta to preheated individual serving bowls. Spoon some tomato sauce over each portion. Add a drizzle of the olive oil and a basil leaf as a garnish. Serve with Parmesan.

Tip: When you buy fresh tomatoes in the winter, if they have a pale, underripe hue to them, keep them in a brown paper bag for a day or two and allow them to ripen at room temperature. The color may not change much, but flavor will improve.

PENNE WITH TOMATOES, ROASTED PEPPERS, AND FRESH ASIAGO CHEESE

4 TO 6 SERVINGS

Fresh tomatoes give this sauce a light, refreshing taste, but you can use canned tomatoes that have been well drained and chopped. Asiago is a mild, semi-soft cheese from the Veneto region of Italy. It is available both aged and fresh. The aged variety is drier, sharper, and saltier than the fresh and can be grated and served as a substitute for Parmesan. The fresh version, my preference, is creamier and melts extremely well. American-made Asiago cheeses are good, but not as good as the imported Italian varieties. In this dish, the Asiago complements the sweet taste of the roasted peppers to perfection.

2 medium-size yellow bell peppers
1 medium-size red bell pepper
2 pounds, approximately 12, medium-size plum tomatoes
1/4 cup olive oil
1 clove garlic, pressed or finely minced
1 tablespoon kosher salt, plus extra for seasoning
2 tablespoons chopped fresh basil leaves
1 tablespoon chopped fresh parsley leaves
1 pound dry penne
1/2 cup grated fresh Asiago cheese

Preheat the oven broiler. Cut the peppers in half lengthwise; remove the seeds, cores, and stems. Place peppers cut side down on an aluminum foil-covered baking sheet. Place under the broiler on the topmost rack; broil until the skins are completely black, about 8 minutes. Remove from the oven, cover loosely with foil, and allow to stand 10 minutes. Under cold running water, use your fingers to gently pull the skins from the peppers. Pat the peppers dry with paper towels. Slice the peppers into $1/4$-inch strips.

Meanwhile, peel the tomatoes. Bring 2 quarts of water to a boil in a large saucepan on top of the stove. Place the tomatoes in the boiling water; cook exactly 1 minute. Drain in a colander and allow to cool slightly. Use a sharp paring knife to cut away the stem end of the tomato and peel off the skin. The skin should slip off easily; if it does not, place the tomatoes back into the boiling water for 30 seconds longer. Cut around the inside core and gently squeeze out the core and seeds. Hold the tomato under cold water to flush out any remaining seeds. Coarsely chop the tomatoes.

Heat the oil in a medium-size skillet over medium-high heat. Add the garlic and tomatoes; season with salt to taste. Cook until the tomatoes begin to give up their juice, 1 to 2 minutes. Reduce the heat to medium-low and simmer about 15 minutes, stirring occasionally. When the sauce is thick, stir in the sliced peppers, basil, and parsley. Cook on the lowest heat about 10 minutes longer.

While the sauce is cooking, bring a large pot of water to a rolling boil over high heat. Add the tablespoon of salt and the penne. Cook, stirring occasionally, until the penne is tender but firm, *al dente*, 7 to 10 minutes. Drain; transfer to a large preheated serving bowl or individual serving plates. Top the pasta with the tomato-and-pepper sauce. Top each serving with some of the Asiago cheese.

LINGUINE WITH TOMATO AND LEEK SAUCE

4 TO 6 SERVINGS

Leeks offer a surprising, tasty change from the customary onions that usually flavor tomato sauces.

$^1/_3$ cup olive oil
2 cloves garlic, pressed or finely minced
3 medium-size leeks (white part only), cut in half lengthwise,
    rinsed well between the layers to remove any sand or dirt,
    and thinly sliced crosswise (to yield 4 cups)
1 tablespoon kosher salt, plus extra for seasoning
$^1/_4$ cup broth (see pages 121–26) or water
2 cups chopped canned tomatoes, with their juice
1 pound dry linguine
Freshly grated Parmesan cheese

Heat the oil in a large skillet over medium-high heat. Add the garlic and leeks; season with salt to taste. Cook, stirring, 1 to 2 minutes until the leeks begin to soften. Reduce the heat to medium-low; cook, stirring occasionally, until the leeks are tender but not brown, about 10 minutes longer. Add the broth and bring to a simmer. Add the tomatoes; stir well to combine. Continue cooking, stirring occasionally, 15 minutes longer until the sauce is thick. Season with salt to taste.

While the sauce is cooking, bring a large pot of water to a rolling boil over high heat. Add the tablespoon of salt and the linguine. Cook, stirring occasionally, until the pasta is tender but firm, *al dente*, 7 to 10 minutes. Drain; transfer to a large preheated serving bowl. Add the sauce; toss well to combine. Serve with Parmesan.

PASTA WITH MUSHROOM SAUCES

When Italians speak of mushrooms, it is always the wonderfully flavorful wild varieties they refer to—white cultivated mushrooms are almost nonexistent in Italy—and that abound in markets throughout the countryside during the damp spring and fall months. Mushroom hunting and gathering is a livelihood for some Italians and a passion for many others, although a limit now exists in some areas as to how much you can gather to protect the natural crop from being depleted.

Mushrooms are called *funghi* in Italian. The most popular and abundant mushroom in Italy is the *porcini* (Boletus edulis). Less available but still enjoyed are *morels* (Morcella esculenta), *oyster mushrooms* (Pleurotus estreatus), and *chanterelles* (Cantharellus cibarius). The most prized *funghi* remain the white and black truffles. Black truffles, *tartufi neri* (Tuber melanosporum), are found mostly in the region of Umbria around Norcia. The pungently aromatic white truffles, *tartufi bianchi* (Tuber magantum), come primarily from the area around Alba in Piedmont and are so closely associated with the area it is called *tartufo d'Alba*.

In recent years, American markets have begun to sell similar varieties of mushrooms, although most are cultivated on specialized mushroom farms, making them available throughout the year. The most common varieties in American supermarkets and specialty greengrocers are the *portobello*, *shiitake*, and *crimini* mushrooms. (The crimini is the variety that was cultivated to become the white button mushrooms so widely available.) Some greengrocers also sell oyster mushrooms, also called *pleurottes*, as well as the pricier morels and chanterelles. In American markets, fresh porcini are rare because they are extremely perishable, although in the future that may change. All these varieties—individually or in a mixture of several varieties—can be used in the recipes in this book.

Dried mushrooms, particularly the dried porcini (or *cepes* as they are called in France) with their intense earthy flavor, are a common ingredient in Italian recipes. Because dried mushrooms are so strong tasting, a little goes a long way. An ounce usually adds enough flavor to a sauce for four people. You also can add some dry mushrooms to fresh white cultivated mushrooms to give them a flavor boost.

When using dried mushrooms, always soak them in very hot or boiling water to cover for at least a 15 minutes before cooking, and drain them well before adding to the recipe. If possible, use the strained soaking liquid in the recipe. (Dried mushrooms often have a lot of dirt and grit on them that is deposited in the soaking water and must be strained out before the liquid can be used.) To strain the liquid, pour through a strainer lined with a double thickness of paper towel.

Tips on Cooking Mushrooms

• Store mushrooms in a paper bag—never plastic—or in a colander in the refrigerator. Mushrooms decompose fairly quickly after being harvested, and moisture speeds up the process significantly, so keep them as dry as possible.

• To clean mushroom caps, use a damp paper towel and wipe the caps to remove any dirt. Never rinse mushrooms under running water. They are highly absorbent, and the water will spoil their texture and make them spongy. You don't have to be concerned about every speck of dirt on the mushrooms if some should get into your food while cooking. Dirt on cultivated mushrooms is usually sterilized, and a little won't adversely affect your health.

• Portobello mushrooms give the best flavor to a dish when the gills on the underside of the cap are trimmed away. Cut away and discard the stems (or reserve for another use); cut the caps in half across; and use a small, sharp paring knife to trim the gills just at the point where they meet the caps. When gills are left on the mushroom, they tend to turn the sauce an inky black color and lend a slightly bitter taste.

• The distinctive flavor of grated Parmesan cheese is not always compatible—and therefore not always served—with mushroom sauces. Always taste the pasta first and then decide if cheese is called for.

MANY MUSHROOM SAUCE WITH LINGUINE

4 TO 6 SERVINGS

Use a mixture of as many different varieties of mushrooms as you can find, such as portobello, shiitake, crimini, white, and especially some dried porcini, which gives a strong, earthy, and very mushroomy flavor to the sauce.

1 ounce dried porcini, or other dried mushrooms
1 cup boiling water
½ cup olive oil
2 tablespoons finely chopped onion
1 large clove garlic, pressed or finely minced
½ pound mushrooms (shiitake, white, or crimini), stemmed, and caps thinly sliced (to yield 2 cups)
½ pound portobello mushrooms, stemmed, and caps thinly sliced (to yield 2 cups)
1 tablespoon kosher salt, plus extra for seasoning
Freshly ground black pepper
1 tablespoon tomato paste
½ cup broth (see pages 121–26)
1 pound dry linguine
2 tablespoons unsalted butter
¼ cup chopped fresh parsley leaves
Freshly grated Parmesan cheese

Place the dried porcini in a heat-proof container. Cover with the boiling water and allow to stand at least 15 minutes. Drain the mushrooms, coarsely chop, and set aside. Strain the liquid through a double thickness of paper towels and reserve.

Heat the oil in a large skillet over medium-high heat. Add the onion and garlic; cook until the onion begins to soften, about 2 minutes. Add the sliced fresh mushrooms; season with salt and pepper to taste, and cook until they begin to soften and start to give up their liquid, about 3 minutes. Stir in the reconstituted dried mushrooms and 2 tablespoons of the soaking liquid. Reduce the heat to medium; cook until the mushrooms are tender, about 7 minutes longer. Stir in the tomato paste and broth. Simmer slowly until the sauce is thick, about 10 minutes longer.

Meanwhile bring a large pot of water to a rolling boil over high heat. Add the tablespoon of salt and the linguine. Cook, stirring occasionally, until the pasta is tender but firm, *al dente*, 7 to 10 minutes. Drain; transfer to a preheated large serving bowl.

Add the butter to the mushroom sauce; cook over medium-low heat until it melts and is combined with the sauce. Stir in the parsley; pour over the pasta. Serve with Parmesan.

BOW TIES WITH PORTOBELLO MUSHROOMS, RADICCHIO, AND MASCARPONE

4 SERVINGS

This richly flavored dish is elegant enough for your fanciest occasions, but also fast and easy. For an even richer dish, use egg fettucine or linguine.

1/4 cup olive oil
2 tablespoons unsalted butter
1/2 pound portobello, crimini, or shiitake mushrooms, stems cut away and caps thinly sliced
1 tablespoon kosher salt, plus extra for seasoning
Freshly ground black pepper
1 clove garlic, pressed or finely minced
1 cup shredded radicchio
1/3 cup mascarpone cheese
1/4 cup freshly grated Parmesan cheese, plus extra for serving
1/4 cup chopped fresh parsley leaves
1/2 pound dry bow ties

Heat the olive oil and butter in a large skillet over medium heat. Add the mushrooms and salt and pepper to taste. Cook, stirring frequently until the mushrooms are tender, 7 to 10 minutes. Add the garlic and radicchio; season lightly with salt. Cook until the radicchio is tender and its bright red color fades to rusty rose, 3 to 5 minutes longer. Turn off the heat. Stir in the mascarpone, Parmesan, and parsley. Set aside.

While the mushrooms are cooking, bring a large pot of water to a rolling boil over high heat. Add the tablespoon of salt and the bow ties. Cook, stirring frequently, until the pasta is tender but firm, *al dente*, 7 to 10 minutes. Drain; transfer to the skillet with the mushroom and radicchio mixture. Turn the heat to low; toss until the cheeses and vegetables are well combined with the pasta. Transfer to a large preheated serving bowl. Season with more salt to taste. Serve with more grated Parmesan.

BOW TIES WITH WILD MUSHROOMS, FRESH SPINACH, AND BUTTERNUT SQUASH

4 SERVINGS

A hearty fall dish with a striking color combination, this recipe was inspired by a mushroom lasagna I enjoyed at the Boston restaurant, Rocco's. In this simplified version, I've tried to retain the irresistible combination of flavors that were unforgettable in the original.

1/3 cup plus 2 tablespoons olive oil
1/2 pound fresh mushrooms (portobello, crimini, or shiitake), stemmed and caps thinly sliced

1 tablespoon kosher salt, plus extra for seasoning
Freshly ground black pepper
2 cups peeled, seeded, and cubed butternut squash
$^1/_2$ pound dry bow ties
1 large clove garlic, pressed or finely minced
3 cups packed fresh spinach leaves, rinsed well in several
    changes of cold water, stemmed, and coarsely chopped
Freshly grated Grana cheese

Heat $^1/_3$ cup of the oil in a medium-size skillet over medium-high heat. Add the mushrooms; season with salt and pepper to taste. Cook, stirring, until the mushrooms are tender, 7 to 10 minutes. Turn off the heat and set aside.

In a separate skillet, heat the remaining 2 tablespoons of olive oil over medium-low heat. Add the butternut squash; season with salt and pepper. Cook, stirring frequently, until lightly browned and tender, about 15 minutes. Turn off the heat; set aside.

Bring a large pot of water to a rolling boil over high heat. Add the tablespoon of salt and the bow ties. Cook, stirring occasionally, until the pasta is tender but firm, *al dente*, 7 to 10 minutes. Drain; transfer to a large preheated serving bowl.

While the pasta is cooking, return the mushrooms to the stove over medium-high heat. Add the garlic and spinach; cook until the spinach is wilted and cooked through, about 5 minutes. Pour the mushroom-and-spinach mixture over the pasta. Top with the butternut squash; toss before serving. Serve with the grated Grana.

PENNE RIGATE WITH PORTOBELLO MUSHROOMS AND FRESH TOMATOES

4 SERVINGS

The Italians would call this dish *al bosco*, which means "from the woods," because it captures the essence of the woodsy flavor of mushrooms, and the tomatoes enhance the earthy taste. This is one of my family's favorite dishes.

8 fresh plum tomatoes
$\frac{1}{2}$ cup olive oil
1 pound portobello, shiitake, or crimini mushrooms,
    stems cut away and caps sliced as thinly as possible
1 tablespoon kosher salt, plus extra for seasoning
Freshly ground black pepper
2 cloves garlic, pressed or finely minced
$\frac{1}{2}$ pound dry penne rigate
$\frac{1}{4}$ cup chopped fresh parsley leaves

To peel the tomatoes, bring 2 quarts of water to a boil in a large saucepan on top of the stove. Place the tomatoes in the boiling water and cook exactly 1 minute. Drain and allow to cool slightly. Use a sharp paring knife to cut away the stem end of the tomato and peel off the skin. The skin should slip off easily. Cut around the inside core with the knife and gently squeeze out the core and seeds. Hold the tomato under cold water to flush out any remaining seeds. Coarsely chop the tomatoes (to yield 2 cups).

Heat the oil in a large skillet over medium heat. Add the mushrooms; season with salt and pepper to taste. Cook, stirring, until the mushrooms are tender, 7 to 10 minutes. Add the garlic and tomatoes; cook, stirring about 5 minutes longer. Turn off the heat; set aside.

Meanwhile bring a large pot of water to a rolling boil over high heat. Add the tablespoon of salt and the penne. Cook, stirring occasionally, until the pasta is tender but firm, *al dente*, 7 to 10 minutes. Drain; transfer to a large preheated serving bowl. Add the mushroom-and-tomato sauce and parsley; toss well. Serve immediately.

✳ SPAGHETTI WITH QUICK MUSHROOM RAGÙ

6 SERVINGS

This is a good, hearty all-purpose sauce that you can prepare with store-bought tomato sauce or with homemade sauce from fresh tomatoes. It is also great for lasagna (see page 200).

3 tablespoons olive oil
½ pound fresh mushrooms (preferably portobello, shiitake, or
    crimini), stemmed, and caps thinly sliced
1 tablespoon kosher salt, plus extra for seasoning
Freshly ground black pepper
1 clove garlic, pressed or finely minced
3 cups Fresh Tomato Sauce (see page 112) or other tomato sauce
1 pound dry spaghetti
Freshly grated Parmesan cheese

Heat the oil in a medium-size skillet over medium-high heat. Add the mushrooms; season with salt and pepper to taste. Cook, stirring gently, until the mushrooms are tender, 7 to 10 minutes. Add the garlic; cook 1 minute longer. Add the tomato sauce; cook 5 minutes to combine the flavors.

Meanwhile, bring a large pot of water to a rolling boil over high heat. Add the tablespoon of salt and the spaghetti. Cook, stirring occasionally, until the pasta is tender but firm, *al dente*, 7 to 10 minutes. Drain; transfer to individual preheated serving bowls. Top each serving with ¹/₂ to 1 cup of the sauce. Serve with Parmesan.

FETTUCINE WITH CREAMY MUSHROOM SAUCE

6 TO 8 SERVINGS

This dish has just enough cream in it to make the sauce deliciously rich without overdoing it—you'll find this pasta is surprisingly light tasting. A little goes a long way, so you can get eight small first course-size portions.

3 tablespoons olive oil
1 pound fresh mushrooms (preferably portobello, crimini, or
    shiitake), stemmed, and caps thinly sliced
1 tablespoon kosher salt, plus extra for seasoning
Freshly ground black pepper
1 clove garlic, pressed or finely minced
2 tablespoons chopped fresh parsley leaves
2 tablespoons unsalted butter
¹/₂ cup light cream or half-and-half
2 tablespoons broth (see pages 121–26)

1 tablespoon mascarpone cheese
1 pound dry or fresh fettucine, spaghetti, or linguine
$^1\!/_2$ cup freshly grated Parmesan cheese, plus extra for serving

Heat the oil in a large skillet over medium heat. Add the mushrooms; season with salt and pepper to taste. Cook, stirring gently,
until the mushrooms are tender, 7 to 10 minutes. Add the garlic;
cook 1 minute longer. Stir in the parsley. Turn off the heat and set
aside.

In a large saucepan, combine the butter, cream, and broth. Simmer, whisking gently, over medium heat until the mixture thickens
slightly, about 10 minutes. Stir in the mascarpone. Turn off the
heat and set aside.

Meanwhile, bring a large pot of water to a rolling boil over high
heat. Add the tablespoon of salt and the fettucine. Cook, stirring
occasionally, until the pasta is tender but firm, *al dente*, 7 to 10 minutes. Drain; transfer to the saucepan with the cream mixture.
Reduce the heat to low. Add the mushrooms and the Parmesan;
cook gently while tossing to combine all the ingredients with the
pasta. Serve in preheated individual bowls with more Parmesan.

PASTA WITH TRUFFLES

It was my good fortune to be in Italy in November—truffle season—while working on this book. I was visiting Umbria, a region rich in truffles. Italy's black truffles come from the area around the southeastern Umbrian town of Norcia, and Umbrian white truffles come from the medieval jewel of a city, Gubbio. (The majority of Italian white truffles come from Alba in the Piedmont region.) It was difficult to avoid truffles at any meal. Their strong, earthy aroma and intense taste enhanced bruschetta and crostini, a variety of pastas, as well as meats, game, and cured salami.

Fall and early winter are the only times of the year when you can buy fresh truffles, and that is when you can prepare pasta with *tartufi bianchi* or *tartufi neri*, fresh white or black truffles. Depending on the harvest and the *lira*-dollar ratio, the price of truffles varies from year to year. They are always expensive, which invariably makes this pasta a pricey dish. But I think it's worth it at least once a year.

CLASSIC FETTUCINE WITH SHAVINGS OF WHITE TRUFFLES

2 TO 3 SERVINGS

This is the traditional way to enjoy white truffles and pasta. I've sampled it many times over the years and enjoyed it again on my trip to Umbria at the restaurant Il Tartufo in Spoleto. Made with very yellow egg fettucine tossed with butter and Parmesan, the pasta is crowned with a mound of paper-thin shavings of white truffle. A truffle shaving tool—a handheld single blade grater with an adjustable blade to control the thickness of the shavings—is helpful for this dish, but not essential. You can use a sharp vegetable peeler or the single-blade on a standard four-sided grater.

$^1/_2$ pound fresh egg fettucine
1 tablespoon kosher salt, plus extra for seasoning
$^1/_4$ cup ($^1/_2$ stick) unsalted butter
$^1/_3$ cup freshly grated Parmesan cheese
Freshly ground black pepper
50 grams (about 2 ounces) fresh white truffle, shaved
   as thinly as possible

Bring a large pot of water to a rolling boil over high heat. Add a tablespoon of salt and the fettucine. Cook, stirring occasionally, until the pasta is tender but firm, *al dente*, 5 to 8 minutes. Drain. Heat the butter in a large skillet over medium heat until bubbling but not brown. Add the drained pasta and the Parmesan; season with salt and pepper to taste. Toss gently until the butter and cheese are combined with the pasta. Transfer to individual preheated serving bowls. Top each serving with the white truffle shavings.

SPAGHETTI WITH WHITE TRUFFLE SAUCE

4 SERVINGS

This pasta was inspired by a sauce I sampled at the trattoria Etrusca in Orvieto. For this sauce, grate the truffle on a fine, rough grater.

1 tablespoon kosher salt, plus extra for seasoning

$^1/_2$ pound dry spaghetti

$^1/_4$ cup ($^1/_2$ stick) unsalted butter

2 tablespoons extra virgin olive oil

50 grams (about 2 ounces) fresh white truffle, finely grated

2 tablespoons mascarpone cheese

$^1/_3$ cup freshly grated Parmesan cheese, preferably
   Parmigiano-Reggiano, plus extra for serving

Freshly ground black pepper

Bring a large pot of water to a rolling boil over high heat. Add the tablespoon of salt and the spaghetti. Cook, stirring occasionally, until the pasta is tender but firm, *al dente*, 7 to 10 minutes. Drain.

In a large skillet, heat the butter and olive oil over medium heat until the butter is bubbling but not brown. Stir in the grated truffle; cook until heated through, 1 to 2 minutes. Gently stir in the mascarpone and Parmesan; continue cooking until the sauce is thick, about 5 minutes. Add the spaghetti to the skillet; season with salt and pepper to taste. Gently toss to combine with the sauce. Serve with more Parmesan.

SPAGHETTI WITH BLACK TRUFFLE SAUCE

4 SERVINGS

In Umbria, where this dish originates, the sauce is served on ombricelli, thick strands of homemade spaghetti typical of Umbrian cooking. You can use regular spaghetti or thick *perciatelli* to get more of the texture of the original dish.

1 tablespoon kosher salt, plus extra for seasoning
½ pound dry spaghetti or perciatelli
¼ cup olive oil
1 clove garlic, pressed or finely minced
100 grams (about 4 ounces) fresh black truffle, finely grated
Freshly ground black pepper
Freshly grated Parmesan cheese

Bring a large pot of water to a rolling boil over high heat. Add the tablespoon of salt and the spaghetti. Cook, stirring occasionally, until the pasta is tender but firm, *al dente*, 7 to 10 minutes. Drain in a colander.

Meanwhile, heat the oil in a large skillet over medium heat. Add the garlic; cook about 2 minutes, being careful not to let it brown. Stir in the grated black truffle. Cook, stirring gently, about 2 minutes longer. Add the drained pasta; season with salt and pepper to taste. Toss to combine with the sauce. Serve immediately with grated Parmesan.

PASTA SAUCES WITH PESTO

Pesto, fresh basil sauce, requires lots of fresh basil leaves, garlic, pine nuts, salt, and fruity olive oil to give it its characteristic flavor. A traditional Ligurian specialty — Liguria is that area of Italy that includes the Mediterranean coast known as the Italian Riviera and the hills just to the north — pesto has become one of the most popular pasta sauces in all Italy. Ligurians who still prepare it by hand, with a mortar and pestle, like to serve pesto in abundant quantities on all types of pasta, from ordinary spaghetti and fettucine to long, wide strips of pasta called lasagnette and the Genovese specialty, small round disks of pasta imprinted with a decorative stamp called *corzetti*.

Although pesto is often served on fresh pasta in Liguria, the pasta is rarely, if ever, an egg pasta. They prepare their fresh pasta with water, flour, and occasionally a little white wine (see page 12).

✳ FRESH PESTO SAUCE

1 CUP

You can make excellent pesto in a food processor or blender. Pesto sauce is traditionally prepared with grated cheese — Parmesan and pecorino. Although it's unconventional, I have found that pasta with pesto has a fresher taste when the cheese is added to the pasta rather than the sauce. And leaving the cheese out of the pesto makes it possible to freeze the sauce for months or to refrigerate it for several weeks without spoiling it. This basic recipe is an ingredient in the recipes that follow.

2 cups tightly packed fresh basil leaves
2 tablespoons pine nuts
1 large clove garlic, peeled
1 teaspoon salt
$1/2$ cup extra virgin olive oil

Combine the basil leaves, pine nuts, garlic, and salt in a food processor or blender. Process until the mixture is finely minced and just beginning to turn into a paste, about 30 seconds. Scrape the sides down. With the machine running, add the oil in a slow, steady stream. When all the oil has all been added, stop the machine and scrape the sides down again. Continue processing until the mixture is smooth, about 30 seconds longer.

▩ LASAGNETTE AL PESTO

6 SERVINGS

I tasted this preparation for pasta and pesto at a wonderful little trattoria, Da Puny, in the tiny seaside resort of Portofino in Liguria. Served on large oval platters, this dish consists of layers of wide lasagna noodles coated with pesto and topped with a blanket of grated Parmesan cheese. This dish is best if you make your own lasagna noodles with Ligurian Eggless Fresh Pasta (see page 12) but you can also use dry lasagna noodles. Figure three layers of lasagna noodles per serving.

1 recipe Fresh Pesto Sauce (see page 112)
$^1/_2$ pound dry lasagna noodles (about 9)
1 tablespoon kosher salt
$^3/_4$ cup freshly grated Parmesan cheese

Prepare the pesto sauce and set aside. Bring a large pot of water to a rolling boil over high heat. Add the salt and lasagna. Cook, stirring occasionally to prevent the lasagna from sticking together, until the pasta is tender but firm, *al dente*, about 10 minutes. Drain the pasta; rinse with warm water. Separate the lasagna and cut in half to make 18 pieces.

Serve on individual preheated plates. Place one piece of pasta on each plate and coat with pesto sauce. Repeat with two more layers of pasta and pesto. Generously sprinkle each serving with grated Parmesan.

▩ PASTA WITH PESTO AND POTATOES

6 SERVINGS

In Liguria, pesto is often served with *trenette* (flat pasta similar to fettucine, but slightly narrower) over a layer of sliced boiled potatoes. Although potatoes may seem like more starch than you would want in this dish, they are used to line the serving bowl and absorb any excess pesto in the dish. When you finally get to eat the potatoes, when the pasta is all gone, they are a flavorful treat.

$1/2$ pound new red potatoes
1 recipe Fresh Pesto Sauce (see page 112)
1 tablespoon kosher salt
1 pound dry trenette, linguine, or fettucine
$1/3$ cup freshly grated Parmesan cheese, plus more for serving

Place the potatoes in a saucepan with water to cover over medium-high heat. Bring the water to a boil; cook until the potatoes are tender when pierced with a sharp knife, about 20 minutes. Drain; allow to stand until cool enough to handle. Peel the potatoes, slice thinly, and arrange in a single layer in six individual serving bowls. Set aside.

Bring a large pot of water to a rolling boil over high heat. Add the salt and pasta. Cook, stirring occasionally, until the pasta is tender but firm, *al dente*, 7 to 10 minutes. Drain; transfer to a large mixing bowl. Add the pesto sauce and Parmesan; toss well to combine with the pasta. Divide the pasta evenly among the six serving bowls. Serve immediately with Parmesan.

SPAGHETTINI WITH WILD MUSHROOMS, PESTO, AND TOMATO SAUCE

4 SERVINGS

The earthy flavor of the mushrooms, combined with the pesto and fresh tomato sauce, gives this sauce a wonderfully hearty taste. This is a nice dish to serve "family style" from a big serving bowl at the table.

1/4 cup olive oil
1 pound fresh mushrooms (preferably portobello, shiitake,
    or crimini), stemmed, and caps thinly sliced
1 clove garlic, pressed or finely minced
2 cups Fresh Tomato Sauce (see page 86) or other tomato sauce
1 tablespoon kosher salt, plus extra for seasoning
Freshly ground black pepper
1 pound dry spaghettini
1/4 cup Fresh Pesto Sauce (see page 112)
Freshly grated Parmesan cheese

Heat oil in a large skillet over medium-high heat. Add the mushrooms; cook until they begin to soften, 3 to 5 minutes. Add the garlic; continue cooking, stirring occasionally, until the mushrooms begin to brown, about 10 minutes longer. Add the Fresh Tomato Sauce; season with salt and pepper to taste. Cook until heated through. Set aside. Reheat before serving.

Bring a large pot of water to a rolling boil over high heat. Add the tablespoon of salt and the spaghettini. Cook, stirring occasionally, until the pasta is tender but firm, *al dente*, 7 to 10 minutes. Drain; transfer to a large serving bowl. Pour the mushroom-and-tomato sauce over the pasta and top with the pesto. Bring the bowl to the table. Toss before serving. Serve with grated Parmesan.

LINGUINE WITH SPICY TOMATO SAUCE, PESTO, AND BASIL CHIFFONADE

4 TO 6 SERVINGS

Long ago I discovered that a dash of good homemade fresh pesto can deliciously transform even the most ordinary, store-bought tomato sauce. When you use a really good fresh tomato sauce, the results are that much better. Crushed red pepper flakes give this sauce its spicy flavor. The basil chiffonade lends an elegant finishing touch.

1 cup Fresh Tomato Sauce (see page 86)
1/4 teaspoon red pepper flakes
1/2 cup Fresh Pesto Sauce (see page 112)
1/2 cup freshly grated Parmesan cheese, plus extra for serving
1 tablespoon kosher salt
1 pound dry linguine
6 fresh basil leaves, sliced crosswise into fine strips

Combine the tomato sauce with the red pepper in a small saucepan over medium heat; gently simmer until very hot, about 10 minutes. Turn off the heat. Add the pesto and cheese; stir well to combine.

Bring a large pot of water to a rolling boil over high heat. Add the salt and linguine; cook until the pasta is tender, but firm, *al dente*, 7 to 10 minutes. Drain the pasta; transfer to a preheated large serving bowl. Pour the sauce over the pasta; toss well. Garnish with the basil leaves. Serve with Parmesan.

SPAGHETTI WITH ZUCCHINI, SUMMER SQUASH, AND FRESH PESTO SAUCE

6 SERVINGS

This is one of my standard summer recipes. The zucchini adds some color and variety to the pasta and pesto, which we eat almost every other night.

1 pound dry spaghetti
1 tablespoon kosher salt
1/2 pound green zucchini, ends discarded and cut into matchsticks 2 inches long
1/2 pound summer squash, ends discarded and cut into matchsticks 2 inches long
1 recipe Fresh Pesto Sauce (see page 112)
1/3 cup freshly grated Parmesan cheese

Bring a large pot of water to a rolling boil over high heat. Add the spaghetti and salt. Cook, stirring occasionally, about 5 minutes. Add the zucchini; continue cooking until the pasta is tender but firm, *al dente*, 3 to 5 minutes longer. Drain; transfer to a large preheated serving bowl. Add the pesto sauce and Parmesan. Toss well and serve.

Chapter Four

PASTA SOUPS

Hearty, filling, and flavorful, pasta soups are the easiest way to quickly cook up a robust, satisfying meal in a single pot. When served with a salad, some good crusty bread, and well-ripened cheese, pasta soup makes a delicious and nutritionally balanced lunch or dinner any time of year: in the winter, served steaming, bubbly hot, and in the warm weather, served cool or at room temperature.

Pasta soups can be creamy smooth or coarsely textured. Just as with other pasta dishes, the key is to match the pasta shape with the other ingredients. Typically the smallest pasta shapes go best with soups: *orzo* (barley shape), *ditallini* and *tubetti* (very short macaroni), *stelline* (stars), *conchilliate* (baby shells), and *anicini pepe* (peppercorn shape). You also can use alphabets or any other diminutive pasta shape you can find. The creamier the soup texture, the smaller the pasta shape should be.

If the soup is not meant to be served as soon as it is cooked, it will thicken as it cools. Have some extra broth on hand. The pasta absorbs quite a bitof liquid while it cooks. You may want to thin the soup before serving.

BROTH FOR PASTA SOUP

Broth is the base for all the soup recipes, although you can use water if broth is not available. Because it is such an important component of soup, always use a flavorful broth—one you enjoy the taste of—whether it is the kind you prepare yourself from raw ingredients or a ready-made, instant variety.

Broth is technically the term for the cooking liquid that results from the preparation of another dish (for example, a French *pot-au-feu* or Italian *bollito misto*). However, Italian cooks use the term *brodo*, as we use the term *stock*: to describe a flavorful liquid made by cooking water with the bones from beef, chicken, or fish or with vegetables. Traditionally, broth was prepared in earthenware pots and simmered, never boiled, for hours. You can prepare a good broth in 1 to 2 hours, and in a pressure cooker in about 30 minutes.

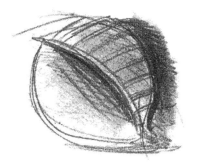

CHICKEN BROTH

ABOUT 12 CUPS

A flavorful chicken broth can be used in any recipe that calls for broth.

3 pounds chicken, whole or parts
2 medium carrots, peeled, cut into quarters
4 ribs celery, ends trimmed, cut into quarters
1 medium onion, peeled
1 small bunch fresh parsley, rinsed in cold water
1 tablespoon kosher salt
3 ½ quarts cold water

Place all the ingredients in an 8- or 10-quart stockpot. Turn the heat to high and bring to a boil. Skim the foam from the top. Reduce the heat to low; simmer, partially covered, for 1½ to 2 hours, until the chicken is falling-off-the-bone tender.

Strain the broth into a large container or bowl and allow to cool. Place in the refrigerator for several hours or overnight so that the fat settles on the top. Skim the fat from the broth with a spoon, and it is ready to be used. It can be stored up to 4 days in the refrigerator or frozen for up to 3 months.

VEGETABLE BROTH

ABOUT 8 CUPS

For vegetarians, or anyone whose diet does not permit a broth made with meat, vegetable broth can be used in any recipe that calls for broth. As with meat or chicken broths, you can make your own or use one of the all-vegetable instant bouillons available.

¼ cup olive oil or other vegetable oil (corn, safflower, but not peanut)
1 large onion, coarsely chopped
1 medium leek, white and green parts rinsed well between the layers to remove any sand or dirt and coarsely chopped
2 medium carrots, peeled and coarsely chopped
2 ribs celery, ends trimmed, coarsely chopped
2 medium-size turnips, peeled and sliced
3 medium-size eating tomatoes, seeded and coarsely chopped
1 small bunch fresh parsley, rinsed in cold water
1 tablespoon kosher salt
1 teaspoon black peppercorns
8 to 10 cups cold water

Heat the oil in a large stockpot over medium-high heat. Add the onion. Cook, stirring, until onion begins to soften, about 2 minutes. Add the leek, carrots, and celery; continue to cook while stirring. Add the turnips, tomatoes, and parsley. Cook until the vegetables begin to brown, about 15 minutes. Add the salt and peppercorns; pour in the water. Turn the heat to high; bring to a boil. Reduce the heat to medium-low. Cover the pot; simmer 1 to 2 hours.

Strain the liquid into a large container or bowl, and it is ready to be used. It will keep in the refrigerator for 4 days and up to 3 months in the freezer.

▣ MEAT BROTH

ABOUT 4 QUARTS

Unlike French stock, which is prepared with well-browned bones and cooked down to almost its essence, this broth is made with meat and bones and is altogether lighter. I recommend preparing a large quantity and freezing it in small containers to have on hand when you need it. Cold water and a few aromatic ingredients make this a most flavorful broth.

2 pounds veal bones
2 pounds chicken backs and necks
1 large onion, peeled
4 ribs celery, ends trimmed, cut into quarters
2 medium carrots, peeled and cut into quarters
1 small bunch fresh parsley, rinsed in cold water
1 tablespoon kosher salt
5 ½ quarts cold water

Place all the ingredients in an 8- or 10-quart stockpot; bring to a boil. Skim the foam from the top of the broth. Reduce the heat to low. Simmer, partially covered, for 2 hours, occasionally skimming the foam from the top.

Strain the broth into a large container or bowl. Let cool slightly and allow to stand in the refrigerator until cold and the fat has settled on top. Remove fat from the broth with a spoon. It can be used immediately, stored in the refrigerator for up to 5 days, or frozen for up to 3 months.

PRESSURE COOKER BROTH

You can use a pressure cooker to prepare chicken, vegetable, or meat broth. Use a 6- or 8-quart pressure cooker for any of the preceding recipes. If you have a 4-quart pressure cooker, reduce the recipes by half. Place the ingredients in the cooker. Add only enough water to fill the cooker two-thirds full. Place the top on the cooker and follow the manufacturer's instructions for using the pressure cooker. Bring the pressure up and allow the broth to cook for 45 minutes for meat; 30 minutes for chicken; and 15 minutes for vegetable broth. Turn off the heat and let the pressure drop gradually. Proceed with the individual recipe.

INSTANT BROTH AND BOUILLON

Instant broth is a useful addition to any pantry. When you don't have the time or the ingredients handy to make fresh broth from scratch, instant or canned broth is an acceptable substitute. It is just as common for Italian cooks at home to use bouillon cubes, called *dadi*, which literally means dice, just as American cooks do. If you want to use instant bouillon, select the brand carefully. Many are salty and flavored with seasonings that give a distinctly artificial taste. Almost all have some preservatives in them. My own preference is for the flavor of the Knorr bouillon cubes. I always overdilute the cubes with 50 percent more water than is called for on the package: 1 cube of bouillon and 3 cups water instead of the 2 cups directed on the package. When using instant broth or boullion, additional salt may not be necessary in the recipe.

BEANS FOR PASTA SOUPS

Beans are the heart of some of the most wonderful pasta soups, *pasta e fagioli*. Beans and dried legumes have been a staple of Italian cooking for thousands of years. Apicius, who documented the eating customs of ancient Rome, described several dishes prepared with dried beans. *Tisanum*, for which he gave the recipe, was a stew of lentils, chick-peas, favas, and barley. During the Renaissance, when beans of all varieties came to be regarded as strictly peasant fare, they fell out of favor with the nobility and aristocracy, although they remained a staple for the majority of Italian people.

Today, the popularity of beans has been firmly established, and they are widely recognized to be delicious, healthful, and economical. Many varieties of beans are popular throughout Italy. Like many other vegetables, however, there are strong regional predilections toward particular beans. For example, lentils are mostly grown in Umbria and are associated with the cooking of that region, whereas chick-peas are almost exclusively grown in the south and are a staple of Abruzzese cuisine.

The most popular beans in Italy include *borlotti*, which are pale pink with red speckles (similar to our pinto beans); *cannellini*, white kidney beans usually associated with Tuscan cooking; chick-peas or *ceci*, which were brought to Italy from the Middle East; brown lentils, *lenticce*, grown in Umbria; and finally *fava* beans, the broad flat beans which, more than any other bean, have long held a special place in Italian culture and cooking. At ancient Roman funerals, favas were presented as an offering to deceased relatives. Favas can be eaten either cooked—fresh or dried—or uncooked, although raw fava beans contain toxins to which some people react and can become ill. Unless favas are very young and small, they should be peeled before eating.

Although dried beans vary greatly in shape, size, and color, they all have a similar nutritional composition: 1 cup of dried beans has approximately 210 calories containing 14 grams of protein; 36 grams of carbohydrates; 0 grams of fat; 4.3 milligrams of iron; 740 milligrams of potassium; with traces of vitamins B1, B2, and B3.

COOKING BEANS

Home-cooked beans have the advantages of tasting better and costing less than store-bought canned beans. With a little advance preparation, you can easily cook your own.

Except for lentils and split peas, beans should be soaked before cooking. This reduces the cooking time by several hours. Place the dried beans in a large bowl, amply cover them with cold water, and allow them to stand, unrefrigerated, 8 hours or overnight. You can cut the soaking time in half if you use boiling water to soak the beans. Always drain and discard the soaking water before cooking the beans.

Beans should be cooked in plenty of water to give them ample room to expand. Exact quantities are not critical because you can add more liquid if necessary. You can cook the beans with a variety of flavorings including onions, carrots, celery, herbs, and garlic. Salt and acidic ingredients, such as tomatoes, should not be added until the beans are almost fully cooked; these ingredients retard the cooking process. I usually cook beans without any flavorings and let them take on the taste of the soup ingredients.

To cook beans in a conventional pot on top of the stove, place the drained soaked beans in a large saucepan or stockpot with 4 cups water for every cup of beans. Place on the stove over medium-high heat and bring to a boil. Reduce the heat to medium-low; simmer, partially covered, until tender. The amount of time it takes to cook different beans depends on the size of the beans, so it follows that the small white beans take less time to cook than the broad fava bean. Approximate cooking times are as follows:

Cannellini (white kidney)	1 to 1 ½ hours
Chick-peas	1 ½ to 2 hours
Fava	1 ½ to 2 hours
Great Northern	1 to 1 ½ hours
Lentils and split peas (unsoaked)	30 to 40 minutes
Pinto beans	1 to 1 ½ hours
Small white (Navy)	¾ to 1 hour

To make sure that the beans are fully cooked, taste to test for doneness.

The fastest way to soak and cook beans is to use a pressure cooker. A pressure cooker cuts the soaking and cooking times dramatically and enhances the natural flavor of the beans because almost nothing cooks away. Always follow the manufacturer's directions for using your pressure cooker, and never fill the cooker more than two-thirds full.

To presoak beans in a pressure cooker, add the beans to the pot with just enough water to cover; close the pressure cooker, according to manufacturer's directions, and bring the pressure up to full. Cook 5 minutes; bring the pressure down immediately by placing the cooker in the sink and running cold water over the top until the safety latches indicate that the pressure has dropped and you can open the top.

To cook beans in a pressure cooker, drain the soaked beans and discard the water. Return the beans to the pot; add 4 cups of fresh cold water for every cup of beans. Follow the manufacturer's instructions for using the pressure cooker and close the cooker. Bring the pressure up to full. Start timing the cooking when the pressure reaches its maximum point, according to the manufacturer's directions. When the cooking time is complete, immediately bring the pressure down by placing the cooker in the sink and running cold water over the top of the pressure cooker. Always drain and rinse the beans well.

Times for cooking beans in the pressure cooker are as follows:

Cannellini (white kidney)	13 to 15 minutes
Chick-peas	20 to 25 minutes
Fava	16 to 22 minutes
Great Northern	14 to 18 minutes
Lentils and split peas (unsoaked)	10 minutes
Pinto beans	14 minutes
Small white (Navy)	12 to 14 minutes

Whether you cook your beans in a conventional pot or in a pressure cooker, in general, you can figure 1 cup of dry beans will yield 2 to 3 cups cooked beans.

If you do use canned beans, always drain and rinse them well in a colander or strainer before cooking.

GENOA-STYLE MINESTRONE WITH TUBETTI AND PESTO

6 SERVINGS

1 medium-size eggplant (about 1 ½ pounds), stem end cut off
  and discarded, and cut into 1-inch cubes
Kosher salt for sprinkling on eggplant and seasoning
⅓ cup olive oil
1 small onion, finely chopped
1 medium-size carrot, finely chopped
1 rib celery, ends trimmed and finely chopped
1 medium-size zucchini, ends discarded and diced
1 small Idaho potato, peeled and diced
8 cups broth (see pages 121–26)
2 cups canned Italian plum tomatoes with their juice
¼ cup packed chopped fresh basil leaves
½ cup dry small elbow macaroni
1 cup dry white kidney beans, cooked according to the directions
  on pages 127–29, or one 16-ounce can cannellini beans, drained
  and rinsed
One 10-ounce package fresh spinach, stems removed, rinsed in
  several changes of cold water, dried, and roughly chopped,
  or one 10-ounce package frozen chopped spinach, cooked
  according to the package instructions and well drained
¼ cup Fresh Pesto Sauce (see page 112)
Freshly grated Parmesan cheese

Place the cubed eggplant in a colander; sprinkle liberally with salt.
Allow to drain at least 30 minutes.

  Heat the oil in a large flame-proof casserole or stockpot over medium heat. Add the onion, carrot, and celery. Cook, stirring, until the onion begins to soften, about 3 minutes. Add the eggplant, zucchini, and potato. Cook, stirring occasionally, about 5 minutes longer. Add the broth, tomatoes, and basil. Increase the heat to medium-high and bring the soup to a boil. Reduce the heat to low; cover and simmer 45 minutes. Add the macaroni; cook 7 minutes longer. Stir in the beans and spinach. Continue cooking until the spinach is cooked and the beans are heated through, about 5 minutes longer. Stir in the pesto; season with salt to taste. Serve with Parmesan cheese.

ANGEL HAIR PASTA IN BROTH WITH FRESH HERBS

6 SERVINGS

This is one of the simplest pasta soups. Make sure that your broth is full of flavor. For a more filling soup, use tortellini in place of the angel hair spaghetti.

1 tablespoon kosher salt
1 pound dry angel hair spaghetti
6 cups broth (see pages 121–26)
1 tablespoon fresh marjoram leaves
1 tablespoon chopped fresh parsley leaves
1 small bunch fresh chives, cut into 2-inch pieces
Freshly grated Parmesan cheese

Bring a large pot of water to a rolling boil over high heat. Add the salt and angel hair pasta. Cook, stirring, until the pasta is tender but firm, *al dente*, 5 to 7 minutes. Drain.

In a large saucepan, heat the broth over medium heat until simmering. When the pasta is ready, add the marjoram and parsley; ladle the broth into individual serving bowls. Place a portion of the pasta in the center of each bowl. Garnish with chives. Serve with Parmesan cheese.

TOMATO SOUP WITH PASTA STARS

6 SERVINGS

This soup has a wonderfully light, fresh taste. Use ripe plum tomatoes, when they're in season, for even more great flavor.

1 large onion, peeled
1 medium-size carrot, peeled
1 clove garlic, peeled
¼ cup olive oil
One 28-ounce can Italian whole tomatoes, drained and coarsely chopped or 3 pounds fresh plum tomatoes, peeled, seeded, and coarsely chopped
4 cups broth (see pages 121–26)
½ cup dry pasta stars or other small pasta shape
1 tablespoon kosher salt
Freshly grated Parmesan cheese

Combine the onion, carrot, and garlic in a food processor; process until very finely chopped, about 10 seconds (or chop by hand). Heat the oil in a large saucepan or 4-quart flame-proof casserole over medium heat. Add the onion, carrot, and garlic. Cook, stirring, until the onion begins to soften, 2 to 3 minutes. Add the tomatoes and broth; bring to a boil. Reduce heat to medium-low;

simmer until the carrots are tender, about 15 minutes. Add the pasta and salt. Continue cooking until the pasta is tender but firm, *al dente*, 10 minutes longer. Serve with Parmesan cheese.

⊞ SPLIT GREEN PEA AND PASTA SOUP

6 SERVINGS

Pasta and split peas make a hearty, satisfying soup that is a wonderful cold weather meal.

3 tablespoons olive oil
1 medium-size onion, finely chopped (to yield about 1 cup)
1 rib celery, finely chopped
1 medium-size carrot, finely chopped
1 clove garlic, pressed or finely minced
1 cup dried split green peas
6 cups broth (see pages 121–26)
½ cup orzo or other small pasta shape
Kosher salt
Freshly grated Parmesan cheese

Heat the oil in a large saucepan over medium-high heat. Add the onion, celery, carrot, and garlic. Cook, stirring, until the onion begins to soften, about 2 minutes. Add the split peas and broth; bring to a boil. Reduce the heat to medium-low. Cover and simmer until the peas are tender and the soup is thick and smooth, 40 to 45 minutes. Raise the heat to medium-high. Stir in the pasta. Cook until the pasta is tender but firm, *al dente*, 7 to 10 minutes longer. Season with salt to taste. Serve with Parmesan cheese.

▓ COUNTRY-STYLE LEEK, POTATO, AND WATERCRESS SOUP WITH ORZO

4 SERVINGS

This is a very low-fat soup, yet it is full of flavor, very hearty, and because of the potatoes, deliciously creamy.

1 large leek (white part only), cut in half lengthwise, rinsed well
    between the layers to remove any sand or dirt, and thinly sliced
    crosswise
½ pound boiling potatoes, preferably Yukon Gold, peeled,
    cut in half, and thinly sliced
4 cups broth (see pages 121–26)
½ cup dry orzo pasta
Kosher salt
1 bunch watercress, thick bottom stems discarded, rinsed
    well in cold water, and roughly chopped (about 2 cups)
Freshly ground black pepper to taste
Freshly grated Parmesan cheese

In a large saucepan, combine the leek, potatoes, and broth. Bring to a boil over high heat. Reduce the heat to medium-low; simmer 15 minutes. Add the orzo; season with salt to taste. Cook 10 minutes longer until the pasta is tender, stirring frequently to prevent sticking. Add the watercress; cook 5 minutes longer. Season with black pepper. Serve with Parmesan cheese.

Variation: Cook the leek and potatoes with the broth as directed above. Add the watercress and cook 5 minutes longer. Puree the vegetables and broth in a food processor, blender, or through a food mill; return the puree to the saucepan. Heat until simmering. Add the orzo. Cook, stirring frequently, 10 minutes. Stir in 2 tablespoons mascarpone cheese (or sour cream or *crème fraiche*) and heat through.

PURÉE OF RED KIDNEY BEANS AND ORZO

6 TO 8 SERVINGS

This soup comes from the Veneto region of Italy where it is typically prepared with barley, called *orzo* in Italian, and served hot in the winter and at room temperature in the summer. I've substituted orzo-shaped pasta for the barley. It is meant to be a very thick soup.

¼ cup olive oil
1 large onion, peeled and finely chopped
1 clove garlic, pressed or finely minced
1 cup dried red kidney beans, cooked according to directions on
    pages 127–29, drained and rinsed, or one 16-ounce can red kid-
    ney beans, drained and rinsed
4 cups broth (see pages 121–26)
½ cup dry orzo
Kosher salt
Freshly ground black pepper
Extra virgin olive oil
Freshly grated Parmesan cheese

Heat the oil in a 4-quart flame-proof casserole or large saucepan over medium heat. Add the onion and garlic. Cook, stirring, until the onion is beginning to turn translucent, about 7 minutes. Add the kidney beans. Cook 5 minutes longer, stirring to make sure that the onions don't burn. Transfer the beans and onions to a food processor fitted with a steel blade or to a blender; process until smooth, about 30 seconds. Pour the beans back into the saucepan. Using a wire whisk, stir in the broth. Place over medium-high heat; bring to a boil. Add the orzo. Reduce the heat to medium-low; simmer until the orzo is tender but firm, *al dente*, about 10 minutes. Stir the soup frequently as it cooks because the orzo tends to stick to the bottom of the pot. Season with salt and pepper to taste. Serve with a drizzle of your best olive oil and some Parmesan cheese.

▨ TUSCAN WHITE BEAN, TOMATO, AND TUBETTI SOUP

4 SERVINGS

In Tuscany, beans are flavored with tomatoes and garlic and cooked, *al fiasco,* in a flask over a wood-burning fire. This soup captures the flavor of the Tuscan original.

2 tablespoons olive oil

1 medium-size onion, finely chopped

2 cloves garlic, pressed or finely minced

1 cup dried small white beans, cooked according to the directions on pages 127–29, or one 16-ounce can cannellini beans, drained and rinsed well

1 cup coarsely chopped canned tomatoes with their juice

3 cups broth (see pages 121–26)

½ cup dry short tube-shaped pasta such as ditallini, tubetti, or macaroni

Kosher salt

¼ cup chopped fresh parsley leaves

Freshly grated Parmesan cheese

In a large saucepan, heat the oil over medium-high heat. Add the onion and garlic. Cook until the onion begins to soften, 2 to 3 minutes. Add the beans, tomatoes, and broth; bring the soup to a boil. Reduce the heat to medium-low; simmer, covered, about 15 minutes. Add the pasta and cook until the pasta is tender but still firm, *al dente,* about 10 minutes longer. Season with salt to taste. Stir in the chopped parsley; serve with Parmesan.

❖ LENTIL AND DITALLINI SOUP

6 SERVINGS

The best and tastiest lentils are the smallest ones. They take longer to cook because they are more compact and dense than larger ones, but they retain their shape and firmness and are much more flavorful. You can use any lentil for this rich-tasting and hearty soup, but if you can find the small Italian lentils from Castelluccio, they make a delicious difference.

⅓ cup olive oil
1 medium-size onion, finely chopped
1 rib celery, finely chopped
2 cloves garlic, pressed or finely minced
1 cup dried lentils, rinsed and picked over
4 cups broth (see pages 121–26)
1 cup chopped canned tomatoes with their juice
Pinch of hot red pepper flakes, or to taste
Kosher salt
½ cup ditallini or other small tubular pasta such as elbow
    macaroni or tubetti
Freshly grated Parmesan cheese

Heat the oil in a large saucepan or 4-quart casserole over medium-high heat. Add the onion, celery, and garlic. Cook until the onion begins to soften, 2 to 3 minutes. Add the lentils and stir in the broth. Bring the liquid to a boil. Reduce the heat to medium-low; simmer until the lentils are tender, 35 to 40 minutes. Add the tomatoes, season with the hot pepper flakes and salt to taste. Add more broth, ½ cup at a time, if the soup seems too thick. Add the pasta. Cook until tender but still firm, *al dente*, about 10 minutes longer. Serve with Parmesan.

✳ PRESSURE COOKER LENTIL AND PASTA SOUP

6 SERVINGS

This is a Barrett family favorite. I've always prepared it in the pressure cooker, but you can easily cook it in a standard pot, although the cooking time will be longer (see preceding recipe).

1 medium-size onion, chopped
2 medium-size carrots, peeled and coarsely chopped
1 rib celery, chopped
3 tablespoons olive oil
2 cups dried lentils, rinsed and picked over
8 cups broth (see pages 121–26)
Kosher salt
1 cup dry tubetti or other small pasta shape
Freshly grated Parmesan cheese

Combine the onion, carrot, celery, and olive oil in a 4- or 6-quart pressure cooker over medium heat. Cook until the onion begins to soften, 2 to 3 minutes. Add the lentils and broth. Close the pressure cooker according to the manufacturer's directions. Turn the heat to high and bring the pressure up to full. When the pressure is up, reduce the heat to medium-low and cook at full pressure for 10 minutes. Turn off the heat. Allow the pressure to drop on its own. Open the cooker according to the manufacturer's directions. Add salt to taste. Turn the heat under the pressure cooker to medium-high; bring the lentil soup to a boil. Add the tubetti; continue cooking, without covering the pot, until the pasta is tender but still firm, *al dente*, about 10 minutes longer, stirring frequently to prevent sticking. Serve with Parmesan.

❊ SOUP OF BORLOTTI BEANS, DRIED PORCINI, AND TUBETTI

4 SERVINGS

Our pinto beans are very much like the Italian *borlotti* beans. The woodsy aroma and flavor of the dried porcini subtly flavors this soup.

2 ounces dried porcini mushrooms (or other dried mushrooms)
1 cup boiling water
3 tablespoons olive oil
1 medium-size onion, peeled and finely chopped
1 clove garlic, peeled and pressed or finely minced
2 cups dried borlotti or pinto beans, cooked according to the
    directions on pages 127–29
1 cup chopped canned tomatoes with their juice
3 cups broth (see pages 121–26)
Kosher salt
½ cup dry tubetti or other small tubular pasta such as ditallini
    or elbow macaroni
Freshly grated Parmesan cheese

Place the mushrooms in a heat-proof glass measuring cup with the boiling water; allow to stand 30 minutes. Strain the mushrooms through a double thickness of paper towels, reserving the liquid, and coarsely chop. You should have about ½ cup chopped mushrooms.

Heat the oil in a medium-size flame-proof casserole or large saucepan over medium-high heat. Add the onion. Cook until the onion begins to soften, 2 to 3 minutes. Add the garlic, beans— mashing some of them against the side of the pot—tomatoes, mushrooms with ¼ cup of their soaking liquid, and the broth. Turn the heat to high; bring the soup to a boil. Reduce the heat to medium-low; simmer until the soup is thick, about 20 minutes. Season with salt to taste. Add the pasta; continue cooking, stirring occasionally, until it is tender but still firm, *al dente*, about 10 minutes longer. Serve with Parmesan.

CHICK-PEAS AND DITALLINI WITH ROSEMARY

6 SERVINGS

Coarsely textured and highly seasoned, this soup of chick-peas and short tube-shaped pasta could almost be a stew.

3 tablespoons olive oil
1 small onion, finely chopped
1 clove garlic, pressed or finely minced
1 cup dried chick-peas, cooked according to the directions
    on pages 127–29, or one 16-ounce can chick-peas, drained and
    rinsed well
1 tablespoon fresh rosemary leaves, coarsely chopped, or
    ¼ teaspoon dried, crumbled
4 cups broth (see pages 121–26)
Pinch of hot red pepper flakes
½ cup dry ditallini or other small tubular pasta shape such as
    tubetti or elbow macaroni
Kosher salt
Freshly grated Parmesan cheese

Heat the oil in large saucepan over medium-high heat. Add the onion and garlic. Cook until the onion begins to soften, 2 to 3 minutes. Add the chick-peas, rosemary, broth, and hot pepper flakes. Bring to a boil. Reduce the heat to medium-low; simmer 10 minutes. Add the pasta. Raise the heat to medium-high; cook, stirring frequently, until the pasta is tender but still firm, *al dente*, about 10 minutes longer. Season with salt to taste. Serve with Parmesan.

THREE BEAN, CABBAGE, AND PASTA SOUP

6 SERVINGS

Colorful and highly flavored, this hearty soup makes a satisfying main course dish.

3 tablespoons olive oil
1 medium-size onion, peeled and finely chopped
1 clove garlic, pressed or finely minced
1 medium-size leek, white part only, cut in half lengthwise, rinsed well between the layers to remove any dirt or sand, and thinly sliced crosswise
1 cup shredded green cabbage, preferably curly-leaf Savoy cabbage
1 rib celery, thinly sliced
2 cups dried beans (a combination of white kidney beans, red kidney beans, and chick-peas), cooked according to the directions on pages 127–29, or canned beans, drained and rinsed
2 tablespoons tomato paste
1 bay leaf
4 cups broth (see pages 121–26)
½ cup dry small tubular pasta such as tubetti, ditallini, or elbow macaroni
Kosher salt
Freshly grated Parmesan cheese

Heat the olive oil in a large saucepan over medium-high heat. Add the onion. Cook, stirring, until it begins to soften, 2 to 3 minutes. Add the garlic, leek, cabbage, and celery; continue cooking until the leek and cabbage are wilted. Add the beans, tomato paste, bay leaf, and broth. Raise the heat to high; bring the broth to a boil. Reduce the heat to medium-low and simmer about 20 minutes, stirring occasionally. Add the pasta. Cook until pasta is tender but still firm, *al dente*, about 10 minutes longer, stirring occasionally. Season with salt to taste. Serve with Parmesan.

WHITE BEAN, PORTOBELLO MUSHROOM, AND ORZO SOUP

6 SERVINGS

¼ cup olive oil

1 small onion, chopped

1 medium carrot, coarsely chopped

1 large clove garlic, pressed or finely minced

½ pound fresh mushrooms (preferably portobello), stemmed, and caps thinly sliced (if caps are very large, cut in half and slice across for smaller pieces)

Kosher salt

4 cups broth (see pages 121–26)

½ cup dry orzo

1 cup dried small white beans, cooked according to directions on pages 127–29, or one 16-ounce can cannellini beans, drained and rinsed well

2 tablespoon chopped fresh parsley leaves

Freshly grated Parmesan cheese

Heat the oil in a large saucepan or 4-quart flame-proof casserole over medium heat. Add the onion, carrot, and garlic. Cook, stirring, until the onion begins to soften, 2 to 3 minutes. Add the sliced mushrooms and season with salt. Continue cooking, stirring, about 3 minutes longer. Pour in the broth and bring to a boil; then lower the heat to medium-low. Cover and simmer 15 minutes. Add the orzo and cook 10 minutes. Add the cooked beans; cook until the orzo is completely tender and the beans are heated through, about 5 minutes longer. Season with salt to taste. Add the parsley; serve with Parmesan.

▦ FAVA, ORZO, AND PESTO SOUP

6 SERVINGS

Fava beans have an intensity of flavor that is unrivaled. This soup is rich and very tasty and hearty enough to be a meal. It thickens as it cools, so have some extra broth on hand to thin it slightly before reheating.

3 tablespoons olive oil
1 medium-size onion, chopped
1 clove garlic, pressed or finely minced
1 cup dried fava beans, cooked according to the directions
    on pages 127–29, or one 16-ounce can fava beans, drained and
    rinsed well
1 cup chopped canned tomatoes with their juice
3 cups broth (see pages 121–26)
½ cup dry orzo
¼ cup Fresh Pesto Sauce (see page 112)
Kosher salt
Freshly grated Parmesan cheese

Heat the oil in a large saucepan or 4-quart flame-proof casserole over medium-high heat. Add the onion. Cook until the onion begins to soften, 2 to 3 minutes. Add the garlic, favas, tomatoes, and 2 cups of broth. Bring the liquid to a boil. Turn the heat to low and simmer about 15 minutes. Transfer the soup to a food processor or blender; process until smooth (you may have to do this in batches). Return the puree to the saucepan. Add the remaining cup of broth and bring the soup to a boil over medium-high heat. Add the orzo. Cook, stirring frequently to prevent sticking, until the orzo is tender but firm, *al dente*, about 10 minutes. Stir in the pesto; season with salt to taste. Serve with Parmesan.

Chapter Five

PASTA SALADS

Pasta salad as we know it — pasta specially cooked and served cold with vegetables, herbs, and dressings or sauces — is an American invention derived from an Italian culinary tradition: during the long hot summers, Italians have always enjoyed pasta — usually left over from the previous night's hot meal — cold or at room temperature.

Because Italian cooking has broken through traditional barriers in Italy as well as here at home, the American concept of pasta salads now has become more popular there. As evidence of that, at least two of Italy's leading pasta manufacturers, Barilla and DeCecco, offer a special pasta just for salads. Barilla calls theirs *Fresca Fantasia,* and it is milled and manufactured to hold up to refrigeration and the weight and moisture of the ingredients and dressing.

You don't have to have special pasta to make a great pasta salad. Any kind of pasta can be combined with crisp fresh or lightly cooked vegetables as well as cheeses, herbs, and savory sauces such as an olive oil-based vinaigrette or a mayonnaise-type dressing. Pasta salads make great dishes to serve large or small crowds for lunch or hot weather dinners, and they provide an easy way for you to use up leftovers. Pasta salad's great appeal is its versatility and ease: you can prepare a pasta salad with little cooking, but an endless list of ingredients.

Pasta Salad Tips

• Short pasta shapes are my favorite for salads. They combine best with the other cut-up ingredients to create a consistent texture. Use bow ties (*farfalle*), corkscrews (*fusilli*), quill shapes (*penne* and *pennette*), wheels (*rotelli*), short, straight macaroni (*tubetti* and *ditallini*), barley shape (*orzo*), shells (*conchiglie*), and little "ears" or discs (*orecchietti*). I suggest a shape for each recipe, but feel free to interchange them, depending on your taste and what you have on hand.

• After draining, rinse pasta for salad in cold water. It helps to stop the cooking process so you can dress and serve it.

• For the best flavor, pasta salads should be dressed while warm or at room temperature, but not hot or cold. You want the pasta to absorb some, but not all, of the dressing. If you dress the pasta while it's hot, it absorbs too much dressing and becomes soft or soggy. If you dress it when it's cold, it won't absorb enough of the flavor of the dressing.

• If possible, use a flavorful extra virgin olive oil to season your salads. It adds a wonderful taste to the dish.

• Always taste and salt the pasta salad after it reaches room temperature. Colder dishes have less flavor than hotter ones.

• Pasta salad should be served at room temperature, not cold from the refrigerator. If you refrigerate the pasta salad, allow it to reach room temperature before serving.

• Use both cooked and raw vegetables in pasta salads. Combinations make for interesting textures and tastes.

• Before serving, toss pasta salads with two large spoons or a spoon and fork to make sure that the dressing that settles on the bottom of the bowl is well combined with the pasta and vegetables.

• Serve pasta salads over a bed of greens: lettuce, mesclun, arugula, and watercress all make a good-looking and good-tasting accompaniment.

• Most pasta salads don't refrigerate well. It's best to prepare and serve pasta salad the same day.

The following recipes all serve at least four people. Depending on what else is being served, you may be able to get more servings per recipe.

▨ PENNE SALAD WITH ROASTED SWEET PEPPERS, HOT JALAPEÑOS, AND BALSAMIC VINAIGRETTE

4 SERVINGS

2 medium yellow bell peppers

1 medium red bell pepper

1 1/2 tablespoons kosher salt

1/2 pound dry penne

1 clove garlic, pressed or finely minced

2 tablespoons balsamic vinegar

1/3 cup extra virgin olive oil

1 red or green jalapeño pepper, stem and seeds removed and
    finely minced

1/2 cup thinly sliced red onion

12 fresh chives, cut into 3-inch lengths

Preheat the oven broiler. Cut the bell peppers in half lengthwise. Remove the seeds and stems and place them cut side down on an aluminum foil-covered baking sheet. Put the peppers under the broiler on the topmost rack; broil until the skins are completely black, about 8 minutes. Remove from the oven; cover loosely with foil. Allow to stand 10 minutes. Under cold running water, use your fingers to gently pull the skins from the peppers. Pat the peppers dry with paper towels. Slice the roasted peppers lengthwise into 1/4-inch strips.

Bring a large pot of water to a rolling boil over high heat. Add 1 tablespoon of the salt and the penne. Cook, stirring occasionally, until the penne is tender but firm, *al dente*, 7 to 10 minutes. Drain; rinse under cold water. Transfer to a large mixing bowl.

Combine the garlic, balsamic vinegar, and the remaining salt in a small bowl; beat lightly with a fork to combine. Continue stirring and add the olive oil in a slow, steady stream. Pour the dressing over the pasta; mix well. Cover lightly with a piece of waxed paper or plastic wrap, stirring the pasta occasionally until it reaches room temperature. Add the bell and jalapeño peppers to the pasta along with the red onion and stir to combine. Before serving, garnish with the chives.

BROKEN SPAGHETTINI SALAD WITH YELLOW PEPPERS, CAPERS, AND LEMONY MAYONNAISE DRESSING

4 SERVINGS

This pasta salad is served as an appetizer, combined with canned tuna, at the restaurant and inn Albergo del Sole in Lombardy in Italy. The broken short strands of spaghettini mean that you don't have to twirl the pasta before eating it.

1 tablespoon plus 1 heaping teaspoon kosher salt
1/2 pound dry spaghettini, broken into thirds
1/2 medium-size yellow bell pepper, stem and seeds removed and thinly sliced
2 tablespoons small capers (if you use large capers, coarsely chop them), drained
1/2 cup sliced red onion
1/2 cup prepared mayonnaise (see note below)
Juice of 1 lemon (1/4 cup juice)

$^{1}/_{2}$ teaspoon Tabasco sauce

2 tablespoons chopped fresh parsley

Bring a large pot of water to a rolling boil over high heat. Add 1 tablespoon of the salt and the broken spaghettini. Cook, stirring occasionally, until the spaghettini is tender but firm, *al dente*, 7 to 10 minutes. Drain the pasta; immediately immerse it in a bowl of ice water to stop the cooking. Allow to stand 1 minute; drain. Transfer the pasta to a large mixing bowl. Add the bell pepper, capers, and onion; toss well.

Combine the mayonnaise with the lemon juice, Tabasco, and remaining salt; beat well with a wire whisk. (If you are using commercially prepared mayonnaise, add less salt and taste for seasoning.) Pour over the pasta and vegetables. Mix well to completely coat the pasta with the dressing. Cover and refrigerate for several hours or overnight. Before serving, taste for seasonings. Garnish with the parsley.

Note: If you can find salmonella-free eggs, you can prepare your own mayonnaise. Combine 1 egg and $^{1}/_{2}$ teaspoon salt in a food processor or blender; process about 30 seconds. With the machine running, gradually pour 1 cup olive oil into the machine in a slow, steady stream. Turn off the machine. Transfer the mayonnaise to a container and refrigerate. It will keep for at least a week in the refrigerator. If you are unsure about your eggs, use store-bought mayonnaise.

Tip: Use a fork to get the most juice out of a half of lemon. Cut a lemon in half crosswise. Insert the fork prongs into the center of the lemon half and squeeze while turning the lemon against the fork. At the same time, gently twist the fork against the lemon.

TUBETTI WITH WHITE BEANS, SPRING ONIONS, AND RADICCHIO

4 SERVINGS

This salad makes an elegant luncheon main course when served with cold grilled vegetables. I like to use small white Great Northern beans, which I quickly cook in the pressure cooker (see pages 128–29). You also can use canned cannellini beans, which should be drained and rinsed well before being added to the salad.

1 cup dried small white beans (Great Northern), cooked
    according to the directions on pages 127–29, or one 16-ounce
    can cannellini beans, drained and rinsed
1 tablespoon kosher salt, plus extra for seasoning
$1/2$ pound dry tubetti or other short pasta
2 tablespoons red wine vinegar
$1/3$ cup extra virgin olive oil
$1/4$ cup chopped fresh parsley leaves
1 clove garlic, pressed or finely minced
Freshly ground black pepper
4 scallions, root end discarded and finely chopped
1 cup shredded radicchio

Drain the beans in a colander and rinse them well. Allow to cool to room temperature.

    Bring a large pot of water to a rolling boil over high heat. Add 1 tablespoon of salt and the tubetti; cook, stirring occasionally, until the pasta is tender but firm, *al dente*, 7 to 10 minutes. Drain; rinse under cold water. Transfer to a large mixing bowl and allow to cool slightly. Add the vinegar, olive oil, parsley, garlic, and salt and pepper to taste. Toss well; let cool to room temperature. Add the beans, scallions, and radicchio; toss well to combine. Serve at room temperature.

Tip: When using parsley, use Italian flatleaf parsley; it's the easiest to chop. Rinse the parsley in several changes of cold water and spin dry. It will keep fresh and crisp in a salad spinner for several days. For easy chopping, pull the leaves from the stalks and mass them together in a pile.

ABOUT RADICCHIO

Radicchio, with its small round shape and purplish red leaves is often confused, at least in the United States, with red cabbage. But one taste and there's no confusing the two vegetables. Radicchio is an endive; it has a distinctly bitter taste but a decidedly tender leaf. Most of the radicchio in the world is grown in the northeastern region of the Veneto in Italy and exported. There are three types of radicchio: the elongated and milder tasting is *radicchio di Treviso*; the round heads, which are the most widely available, are the *radicchio di Chioggia*; the third, variegated red and white, is the *radicchio di Castelfranco*. All three types are used in salads. In Treviso, where much of the radicchio is grown, you'll find many dishes prepared with radicchio, including pastas, risotto, and antipasti.

▨ ORZO SALAD WITH LEMON AND PARSLEY DRESSING

4 SERVINGS

A great accompaniment to many dishes, this versatile salad is also wonderful with cooked vegetables added to it.

$^{1}/_{2}$ pound dry orzo
1 tablespoon kosher salt, plus extra for seasoning
1 cup packed fresh parsley leaves and stems
Juice of $^{1}/_{2}$ lemon (about 2 tablespoons) or more to taste
$^{1}/_{4}$ cup extra virgin olive oil

Bring a large pot of water to a rolling boil over high heat. Add the orzo and 1 tablespoon of salt. Cook, stirring occasionally, until the pasta is tender but firm, *al dente*, 7 to 10 minutes. Drain; transfer to a large mixing bowl. Allow to cool slightly.

Place the parsley in a food processor fitted with the metal blade. Process until finely chopped, about 10 seconds. Add the lemon juice and salt to taste. Continue processing. While the machine is running, add the olive oil in a slow, steady stream. Pour the dressing over the orzo; stir well to combine. Season with more salt and lemon juice to taste. (If you don't have a food processor, chop the parsley by hand; transfer to a small mixing bowl; and stir in the lemon juice, salt, and olive oil.) Serve at room temperature.

RIGATONI WITH GRILLED CAPONATA AND BALSAMIC DRESSING

4 SERVINGS

This salad was inspired by a dish from the restaurant, Al Forno, in Providence, Rhode Island. For convenience, use a stove-top cast-iron grill to prepare the vegetables, or you can fire up your barbecue.

1 medium-size eggplant (about 1 ½ pounds)
1 tablespoon kosher salt, plus extra for sprinkling on eggplant
1 large Vidalia or Spanish onion
Olive oil
½ cup Gaeta or Calamata olives, pits removed and cut into quarters
2 tablespoons small capers or chopped large capers, drained
¼ cup chopped canned tomatoes with their juice
2 tablespoons balsamic vinegar
⅓ cup extra virgin olive oil
½ pound dry rigatoni

Cut the eggplant crosswise into ¾-inch thick round slices; place in a large colander. Sprinkle eggplant with salt and allow to drain for about 30 minutes. Pat dry with paper towels. Preheat the grill. Brush the eggplant slices on both sides with olive oil. Grill 5 to 7 minutes on each side until the slices are tender when pierced with a sharp knife. Slice the onion into ¼-inch thick rounds. Brush the onion slices with olive oil. Grill 5 to 7 minutes on each side until tender when pierced with a sharp knife. Coarsely chop the eggplant and onion; transfer to a large mixing bowl. Add the olives and capers.

In a small mixing bowl, combine the chopped tomatoes, balsamic vinegar, and extra virgin olive oil; set aside.

Bring a large pot of water to a rolling boil over high heat. Add the tablespoon of salt and the rigatoni. Cook, stirring occasionally, until the pasta is tender but firm, *al dente*, 7 to 10 minutes. Drain and rinse under cold water. Add to the mixing bowl with the eggplant mixture. Pour the tomato-and-vinegar dressing over the pasta and vegetables; toss well to combine. Cover lightly with waxed paper and allow to reach room temperature before serving.

ABOUT OLIVES

The olive makes its biggest contribution to Italian cooking in olive oil. But olives are wonderful when added to many salads for their flavor, color, and texture, as well as to eat and enjoy alone. Over three hundred varieties of olives grow throughout the Italian peninsula. Olives are native to the Mediterranean region where they have been cultivated since about 3000 B.C.

To my taste, the best Italian olives for salads are the small, black Gaeta olives, which come from southern Italy and the even smaller Ligurian, Taggiasca olives, which are like the French Nicoise olives but slightly larger. They are not widely available, but can usually be found in bulk or in jars in Italian specialty stores. Greek Calamata, black oil-cured olives, and the tiny French Nicoise olives also can be used in the recipes.

PENNETTE SALAD WITH ROASTED ASPARAGUS, ZUCCHINI, AND LEMON AND PARSLEY DRESSING

4 SERVINGS

$1/2$ pound dry pennette (or penne, rotini, or ziti)

1 tablespoon kosher salt, plus extra for seasoning

1 medium zucchini, about $1/2$ pound, ends discarded, cut into
$1/4$-inch-thick julienne strips

$1/2$ pound skinny asparagus spears, tough bottoms discarded
and spears cut into 3 or 4 pieces, keeping the tips whole

$1/4$ cup plus 2 tablespoons olive oil

2 tablespoons fresh lemon juice

$1/2$ cup packed fresh parsley leaves, chopped

$1/3$ cup chopped fresh chives or scallion greens

Bring a large pot of water to a rolling boil over high heat. Add the pennette and a tablespoon of salt. Cook, stirring occasionally, until the pasta is tender but firm, *al dente*, 7 to 10 minutes. Drain; rinse under cold water. Transfer to a large mixing bowl.

Meanwhile, preheat the oven to 500°F. Combine the zucchini and asparagus in a small roasting pan. Add 2 tablespoons of the olive oil and a sprinkling of salt; toss well to combine. Place on the topmost rack in the oven; roast for 15 minutes. Remove from oven and cool slightly until warm.

Combine the zucchini and asparagus with the pennette; toss well. In a small bowl, mix together the remaining olive oil with the lemon juice and parsley. Pour the dressing over the pasta and vegetables; toss well. Serve at room temperature. Add salt to taste. Garnish with chives.

▨ EGG TAGLIATELLE WITH AVOCADO, FRESH TOMATOES, AND GREEN ONIONS

4 SERVINGS

This recipe was given to me by Barilla Alimentare Dolciaria S.p.A., Italy's largest pasta manufacturers. The avocado makes a deliciously creamy sauce for the cold pasta. For the best appearance, serve this dish soon after dressing it because the creamy green avocado discolors and turns brown when exposed to the air.

1/2 pound dry or fresh egg fettucine
1 tablespoon kosher salt, plus extra for seasoning
1 teaspoon olive oil
1 cup cherry tomatoes, stems removed and seeds squeezed out
2 scallions, root ends discarded, cut into 1-inch pieces
1 ripe avocado, peeled and pit removed
2 tablespoons fresh lemon juice
1 tablespoon extra virgin olive oil
1/2 cup chopped fresh chives or scallion greens

Bring a large pot of water to a rolling boil over high heat. Add the fettucine and a tablespoon of salt. Cook, stirring occasionally, until the pasta is tender but firm, *al dente*, about 5 minutes for the fresh and 7 minutes for the dry. Drain; rinse under cold water. Transfer to a large serving bowl. Add the teaspoon of olive oil; toss the pasta to coat it. Toss occasionally while the pasta cools.

When the pasta is at room temperature, combine the tomatoes and scallions in a food processor fitted with a metal blade, or finely chop by hand. Process for about 15 seconds until finely chopped.

Add the avocado. Pulse the machine on and off until the avocado is almost smooth. Add the lemon juice, extra virgin olive oil, and salt to taste. Turn the processor on and off 2 or 3 times to combine. Add the avocado sauce to the pasta; toss well. Add more salt to taste. Garnish with the chives.

PENNETTE SALAD WITH RED AND YELLOW TOMATO SALSA AND LIME CILANTRO DRESSING

4 SERVINGS

This is a tangy dish with pungent flavors. For a milder taste, cut down on the quantity of hot pepper and use parsley in place of the cilantro. If yellow tomatoes are not available, double the quantity of cherry tomatoes.

$1/2$ pound dry pennette
1 tablespoon kosher salt, plus extra for seasoning
1 teaspoon olive oil
1 cup red cherry tomatoes, stems removed and seeds squeezed out
1 cup yellow cherry tomatoes, stems removed and seeds squeezed out
2 scallions, root ends discarded, cut into several pieces
1 tablespoon chopped green jalapeño pepper, or to taste
$1/4$ cup chopped cilantro (fresh coriander) or parsley leaves
$1/4$ cup extra virgin olive oil
2 tablespoons fresh lime juice

Bring a large pot of water to a rolling boil over high heat. Add the pennette and the tablespoon of salt. Cook, stirring occasionally, until the pasta is tender but firm, *al dente*, 7 to 10 minutes. Drain; rinse under cold water. Transfer to a large serving bowl. Add the teaspoon of olive oil; toss well. Toss occasionally until the pasta is room temperature.

While the pasta is cooling, combine the cherry tomatoes, scallions, jalapeño, and cilantro in a food processor fitted with the metal blade. Turn the processor on and off several times until the contents are coarsely chopped. Be careful not to overprocess the tomatoes. Transfer the tomato mixture to a wire mesh strainer, season lightly with salt, and allow to drain, stirring occasionally for 30 minutes. Transfer the tomato mixture to a small mixing bowl. Add the extra virgin olive oil and lime juice; mix well with a fork. Pour over the pennette. Add more salt to taste. Toss the pasta salad well before serving.

PENNE AND GRILLED VEGETABLE SALAD WITH BASIL DRESSING

4 SERVINGS

The grilled, charred flavor of the vegetables really comes through in this salad. Slice the vegetables thinly so they'll cook quickly on your barbecue or stove-top grill.

$\frac{1}{2}$ pound dry penne

1 tablespoon kosher salt, plus extra for sprinkling on eggplant

2 tablespoons plus 1 teaspoon olive oil

1 small eggplant, about $\frac{1}{2}$ pound, stem end discarded, cut crosswise into $\frac{1}{4}$-inch thick round slices

2 to 3 small zucchini, about $\frac{1}{2}$ pound, ends discarded and sliced on the diagonal $\frac{1}{8}$-inch thick

1 medium red bell pepper, cut in half, stem and seeds removed
and each half cut into 6 pieces
1 medium-size onion, peeled and sliced 1/4-inch thick
1 medium-size carrot, thinly sliced on the diagonal
8 oil-packed sun-dried tomato halves, drained and sliced
lengthwise into strips
1/4 cup extra virgin olive oil
1 teaspoon red wine vinegar
1 clove garlic, pressed or finely minced
1 tablespoon chopped fresh basil
1 tablespoon chopped fresh parsley

Bring a large pot of water to a rolling boil over high heat. Add the penne and the tablespoon of salt. Cook, stirring occasionally, until the pasta is tender but firm, al dente, 7 to 10 minutes. Drain; rinse under cold water. Transfer to a large serving bowl. Add 1 teaspoon of the olive oil; toss well. Toss occasionally while the pasta cools.

Prepare the barbecue for grilling or preheat a cast-iron grill on top of the stove. Place the eggplant in a colander; sprinkle lightly with salt. Allow to drain while you grill the other vegetables. Combine the zucchini, red pepper, onion, and carrot in a large mixing bowl. Toss with the remaining olive oil. Grill all the vegetable pieces on both sides until tender, 5 to 7 minutes on each side. Add the eggplant to the bowl after patting it dry with paper towels. Toss with the olive oil and grill on both sides until tender, 5 to 7 minutes. Cut the eggplant slices into quarters. Add all the grilled vegetables and the sun-dried tomatoes to the penne; toss well.

When the penne and vegetables reach room temperature, combine the extra virgin olive oil, vinegar, garlic, basil, and parsley in a small nonaluminum mixing bowl; mix well. Add to the pasta and vegetables. Toss well to combine and serve.

SALAD OF BOW TIES, FRESH FENNEL, CHICK-PEAS, AND PECORINO

4 SERVINGS

$^1/_2$ pound dry bow ties

1 tablespoon kosher salt, plus extra for seasoning

1 teaspoon olive oil

1 small bulb fresh fennel (about $^1/_2$ pound), tall stalks and leaves discarded (or reserved for another use) and bulb sliced as thinly as possible, preferably in a food processor or on a mandoline

1 medium-size red onion, peeled and thinly sliced (about 1 cup)

1 cup dried chick-peas, cooked according to the directions on pages 127–29, or one 16-ounce can chick-peas, rinsed well and drained

$^1/_2$ cup extra virgin olive oil (approximately)

1 tablespoon red wine vinegar

Freshly ground black pepper

Bring a large pot of water to a rolling boil over high heat. Add the bow ties and salt. Cook, stirring occasionally, until the pasta is tender but firm, *al dente*, 7 to 10 minutes. Drain; rinse under cold water. Transfer to a large mixing bowl. Add the olive oil; toss well, allow to cool.

In a small mixing bowl, combine the fennel, onion, and chick-peas. Add the extra virgin oil, vinegar, and salt and pepper to taste. Stir to combine. When the pasta has cooled, add the vegetables and seasonings; toss well. Serve at room temperature.

▓ FUSILLI SALAD WITH SUN-DRIED TOMATOES AND BROCCOLI

4 SERVINGS

$\frac{1}{2}$ pound dry fusilli, rotini, or cavatappi
1 tablespoon kosher salt, plus extra for seasoning
1 cup oil-packed sun-dried tomato halves, drained
2 tablespoons oil from the sun-dried tomatoes
2 tablespoons extra virgin olive oil
1 bunch broccoli, heavy stalks discarded and tops cut into
   bite-size florets (to yield 3 to 4 cups)
2 scallions, root ends discarded, chopped

Bring a large pot of water to a rolling boil over high heat. Add the fusilli and salt. Cook, stirring occasionally, until the pasta is tender but firm, *al dente*, 7 to 10 minutes. Drain in a colander and allow to cool.

Meanwhile, combine the sun-dried tomatoes and the oil from the tomatoes in a food processor fitted with a metal blade. Process until the tomatoes are finely chopped, about 30 seconds. (You can also chop the tomatoes by hand and then combine them with the oil in a small bowl.) Steam or boil the broccoli until tender, about 5 minutes. Rinse broccoli under cold water; set aside to cool completely.

When the pasta has cooled to lukewarm, transfer it to a large mixing bowl. Add the chopped sun-dried tomatoes, extra virgin olive oil, and broccoli. Add salt to taste sparingly—the sun-dried tomatoes are usually sufficiently salty. Toss well to combine. Garnish with the chopped scallions. Serve at room temperature.

SALAD OF BOW TIES, SPICY MARINATED ARTICHOKE HEARTS, AND OLIVES

4 SERVINGS

I recommend using frozen artichoke hearts for this recipe because they require so little preparation: they can be defrosted but don't need any cooking. For the most flavor, marinate them overnight.

One 9-ounce package frozen artichoke hearts, defrosted and
    each sliced lengthwise into 2 to 3 pieces
1 large clove garlic, pressed or finely minced
Pinch of red pepper flakes, or to taste
$1/4$ cup chopped fresh parsley leaves
$1/4$ cup extra virgin olive oil and more as needed
Juice of $1/2$ lemon (about 2 tablespoons)
Freshly ground black pepper
1 tablespoon kosher salt, plus extra for seasoning
$1/2$ pound dry bow ties
1 small red bell pepper, stem and seeds removed and thinly
    sliced lengthwise (about 1 cup)
$1/2$ cup Gaeta or Calamata olives, pitted and cut in half

In a small nonaluminum bowl, combine the artichoke hearts with the garlic, red pepper flakes, parsley, olive oil, and lemon juice. Season with pepper and salt to taste. Stir to combine. Cover and allow to stand at room temperature for several hours or overnight.

Bring a large pot of water to a rolling boil over high heat. Add the tablespoon of salt and bow ties. Cook, stirring occasionally, until the pasta is tender but firm, *al dente*, 7 to 10 minutes. Drain in a colander and allow to stand until lukewarm.

Place the pasta in a large mixing bowl. Add the marinated artichoke hearts, sliced red pepper, and olives. Toss well to combine. Add salt and more olive oil to taste. Stir well before serving. Serve at room temperature.

SALAD OF BOW TIES WITH MARINATED MUSHROOMS, ARUGULA, AND SHAVINGS OF PARMIGIANO-REGGIANO

4 SERVINGS

You can use any mushroom or a mixture of different mushrooms in this recipe. I like to use portobello and crimini because they have a lot more flavor than ordinary white mushrooms.

$^1/_2$ pound fresh mushrooms, stemmed, caps wiped clean,
    and thinly sliced (about 2 cups sliced)
$^1/_3$ cup extra virgin olive oil
Juice of 1 lemon (about 4 tablespoons)
1 clove garlic, pressed or finely minced
Freshly ground black pepper
1 tablespoon kosher salt, plus extra for seasoning
$^1/_2$ pound dry bow ties
1 bunch arugula, stems discarded and coarsely chopped
    (about 2 cups chopped)
One 3-ounce piece Parmigiano-Reggiano cheese

In a medium-size nonaluminum mixing bowl, combine the mushrooms with the olive oil, 2 tablespoons of the lemon juice, and pepper and salt to taste. Stir well. Cover and allow to stand, unrefrigerated, until the mushrooms are tender, 1 to 2 hours.

Bring a large pot of water to a rolling boil over high heat. Add the tablespoon of salt and bow ties. Cook, stirring occasionally, until the pasta is tender but firm, *al dente*, 7 to 10 minutes. Drain; transfer to a colander to cool.

When the pasta is room temperature, place it in a large serving bowl. Add the mushrooms and arugula; toss well. Taste and add more lemon juice, olive oil, and salt as needed. Use a vegetable peeler to shave strips of the cheese onto the pasta. Toss well before serving.

PENNE SALAD WITH FRESH TOMATOES, MOZZARELLA, AND SPINACH

4 SERVINGS

The classic tomato and mozzarella salad, *Insalata Caprese,* was the inspiration for this recipe. The steamed spinach adds nice flavor and color to the dish.

½ pound dry penne

1 tablespoon kosher salt, plus extra for seasoning

2 cups fresh spinach leaves, stemmed, rinsed well in several changes of water but not dried, and coarsely chopped

¼ cup plus 1 tablespoon extra virgin olive oil

1 cup red cherry tomatoes, stemmed, seeds squeezed out, and cut in half

4 ounces fresh mozzarella cheese, preferably mozzarella di bufala (buffalo's milk mozzarella or other fresh-made mozzarella), cut into 1-inch pieces

2 tablespoons chopped fresh basil leaves

Bring a large pot of water to a rolling boil over high heat. Add the penne and salt. Cook, stirring occasionally, until the pasta is tender but firm, *al dente,* 7 to 10 minutes. Drain in a colander and allow to cool to room temperature.

Place the spinach in a small saucepan over medium-high heat. Cover and cook until the spinach is completely wilted and tender, about 5 minutes. Drain; transfer to a small bowl. Add 1 tablespoon of the olive oil and a sprinkling of salt. Allow to cool to room temperature.

When the pasta is cool, transfer to a large serving bowl. Add the tomatoes, mozzarella, spinach, basil, and the remaining olive oil; toss well to combine. Allow to stand at least an hour, unrefrigerated. Toss well before serving.

ORECCHIETTE SALAD WITH LENTILS AND SWEET CORN

4 SERVINGS

Pasta and lentils make a hearty, satisfying salad that can easily be a main dish. The corn adds a refreshing, sweet flavor. Serve this salad on a bed of bitter greens.

$1/2$ cup dried lentils, picked over and rinsed
4 cups water
1 small red onion, peeled and quartered
1 medium carrot, peeled and cut into 2-inch pieces
1 rib celery, ends trimmed and cut into 2-inch pieces
1 tablespoon kosher salt, plus extra for seasoning
Freshly ground black pepper
$1/4$ cup extra virgin olive oil
$1/4$ cup chopped fresh parsley leaves
$1/2$ pound dry orecchiette
2 cups cooked corn or one 10-ounce package frozen corn,
    defrosted

Put the lentils in a small saucepan with the water and place over medium-high heat. When the water boils, cover the pot and reduce the heat to low. Simmer until the lentils are tender, about 35 minutes. Drain; rinse with cold water. Transfer to a small mixing bowl to cool.

Combine the onion, carrot, and celery in a food processor fitted with a metal blade. Pulse the machine on and off until the vegetables are finely chopped (or chop by hand). Add the vegetables to the lentils. Season with salt and pepper to taste. Add the olive oil and parsley; stir to combine. Set aside.

Bring a large pot of water to a rolling boil over high heat. Add the orecchiette and the tablespoon of salt. Cook, stirring occasionally, until the pasta is tender but firm, *al dente*, 8 to 10 minutes. Drain and allow to cool to room temperature. Transfer to a large serving bowl. Add the lentil mixture; stir well to combine. Season with more salt and olive oil to taste. Allow to stand at least an hour, unrefrigerated. Toss well before serving.

SALAD OF BOW TIES, RED POTATOES, AND MUSTARD VINAIGRETTE DRESSING

4 SERVINGS

Pasta and potatoes complement each other and make a satisfying, great-tasting salad. Fresh scallions and mustard dressing add a sharp, palate-pleasing accent.

$\frac{1}{2}$ pound small red potatoes, sliced $\frac{1}{4}$-inch thick
$\frac{1}{2}$ pound dry bow ties
1 tablespoon kosher salt, plus extra for seasoning
1 tablespoon Dijon mustard
$\frac{1}{4}$ cup extra virgin olive oil or more to taste
1 teaspoon red wine vinegar
3 scallions, root ends removed and finely chopped ($\frac{1}{2}$ cup)
Freshly ground black pepper

Place the sliced potatoes in a small saucepan fitted with a steamer basket and steam over boiling water until tender, 7 to 10 minutes. Remove and allow to cool slightly.

Bring a large pot of water to a rolling boil over high heat. Add the bow ties and salt. Cook, stirring occasionally, until the pasta is tender but firm, *al dente*, 7 to 10 minutes. Drain; transfer to a large serving bowl to cool slightly.

When the pasta and potatoes have cooled to lukewarm, combine them in the serving bowl and gently mix with a wooden spoon or your hands, being careful not to break the potatoes. Combine the mustard, oil, and vinegar in a small mixing bowl with a wire whisk and beat until smooth and thick. Season the pasta and potatoes with salt and pepper to taste; pour the mustard dressing over them. Toss to combine. Garnish with the scallions and serve at room temperature.

LEMONY LINGUINE SALAD WITH SUGAR SNAP PEAS AND FRESH HERBS

4 SERVINGS

If you can find lemon linguine, it gives an added boost of flavor to this dish. Plain linguine is also fine, but you may want to add more lemon juice before serving.

1/2 pound fresh lemon linguine or plain dry linguine
1 tablespoon kosher salt
1/2 cup extra virgin olive oil
Juice of 1 lemon (about 4 tablespoons), or to taste
1/2 pound fresh sugar snap peas, ends trimmed
1/2 cup chopped mixed fresh herbs, including chives, or the greens
   from scallions, tarragon, basil, parsley, and marjoram

Bring a large pot of water to a rolling boil over high heat. Add the linguine and salt. Cook, stirring occasionally, until the pasta is tender but firm, *al dente*, 5 minutes (or longer if you are using dry pasta). Drain; transfer to a large serving bowl. Allow to cool slightly.

Combine the olive oil and lemon juice in a small bowl; stir well with a fork. Pour over the pasta. Season with salt to taste and toss well. Allow to cool to room temperature.

Meanwhile, bring a small saucepan of water to boil over high heat. Add the sugar snap peas and cook exactly 1 minute. Drain; rinse under cold water to stop the cooking. Allow to cool to room temperature. Add the peas to the pasta along with the chopped fresh herbs; toss well to combine. Season with more salt and lemon juice to taste.

PENNE SALAD WITH STRING BEANS, RED ONIONS, AND TOMATO VINAIGRETTE

4 SERVINGS

String beans and penne are a perfect match. Cut the beans on a diagonal to be the same length and shape as the penne. You can also add other steamed vegetables to this salad.

1 cup water
$\frac{1}{2}$ pound string beans, tips trimmed and cut in half diagonally
1 tablespoon kosher salt, plus extra for seasoning
$\frac{1}{2}$ pound dry penne
1 small red onion, peeled, cut in half and sliced as thinly as
   possible
$\frac{1}{4}$ cup chopped canned tomatoes, with their juice
$\frac{1}{2}$ cup extra virgin olive oil
1 clove garlic, pressed or finely minced
1 tablespoon chopped fresh parsley leaves
1 tablespoon red wine vinegar
Freshly ground black pepper

Put the water in a 2-quart saucepan fitted with a steamer basket and bring to a boil over medium-high heat. Add the string beans. Cover and cook 8 minutes, or until tender. Drain the beans; rinse under cold water to stop the cooking. Set aside.

Bring a large saucepan of water to a rolling boil over high heat. Add the salt and penne. Cook, stirring occasionally, until the pasta is tender but firm, *al dente*, 7 to 10 minutes. Drain; rinse under cold water. Transfer to a large serving bowl. Add the string beans. Toss occasionally until the pasta and beans have cooled to room temperature. Add the onions; stir to combine.

In a small nonaluminum mixing bowl, combine the chopped tomatoes, oil, garlic, parsley, and vinegar; stir with a wire whisk to combine. Season the pasta with salt and pepper to taste. Pour the dressing over the pasta salad. Toss well and serve.

Chapter Six

BAKED AND FILLED PASTA WITH VEGETABLES

Few foods, to my taste, are as heart- and soul-warming as baked pasta. Dishes that come hot and bubbling from the oven, filled with tender pasta sheets or shapes, fresh seasonal vegetables, creamy cheeses, and satisfying sauces are the consummate comfort food. Baked pasta also happens to be an ideal one-dish main course meal and the most convenient—and among the most elegant—for a buffet dinner. You can prepare baked pasta dishes well in advance and have them warming in the oven while you attend to your own affair—be it simple or simply grand.

The ancient Romans, with their complicated cooking and elaborate entertaining practices, created the first lasagna. Called *laganum* in Latin, it was a dish prepared with sheets or strands of dough baked together with other ingredients. The evolution of lasagna and other baked pasta dishes reached its height during the Italian Renaissance when increasingly complex dishes were served at the ornate meals that became an integral part of the life of the nobility. Baking ovens were a rarity for most people (the common folk communally shared the bakers' ovens in the towns), but the aristocracy were able to build ovens in their villas and estates and prepared these abundant and involved dishes to impress their guests. And as far as they were concerned, there was no limit as to what could be baked together into these pasta concoctions—meats, game, eggs, cheeses—the more fantastic the better.

Today, lasagna and baked pasta of all kinds are found throughout the Italian peninsula—every region has its specialties and characteristic preparations. In Emilia-Romagna, you'll find the classic tomato and meat sauce lasagna layered with a creamy white sauce and cheeses; whereas in southern Italy, a lasagna is typically prepared with regional ingredients such as meatless tomato sauce, mozzarella, and ricotta. And although the fantasy of the Renaissance dishes may be gone, baked pastas can still be fantastic creations that are hearty and satisfying and most of all delicious.

Fresh pasta adds an extraordinary dimension of texture and flavor to lasagna and cannelloni. As with any homemade fresh pasta dish, you'll find fresh pasta in these preparations practically melts in your mouth, taking the dish from the ordinary and moving it into the realm of the truly heavenly. Time and convenience, however, usually lead most cooks to dry lasagna noodles and preformed cannelloni (also called *manicotti*) cases. As with all pasta, when it comes to choosing dry pasta for lasagna or cannelloni, the best are the Italian-made lasagna noodles or sheets. They are significantly thinner and more delicate than their American-made counterparts, in addition to having the characteristic flavor and texture that distinguishes Italian-made pasta.

Though some of the Italian lasagna pastas—Barilla and Delverde to name two—say they don't require any precooking when baked into a lasagna, I find they work best when partially cooked for approximately 5 minutes. This softens them, makes them pliable enough to roll into cannelloni, and when baked, allows them to fully meld with the sauce, cheeses, and vegetables.

ABOUT CHEESES

Italian fontina and mozzarella are the best melting cheeses. You can use other good melting cheeses in these recipes, such as Emmenthaler, Gruyère, bel paese, taleggio, and robiola.

About mozzarella: Naples and the region around it are known for mozzarella cheese. Although most mozzarella is made from cow's milk, the best (and consequently the most expensive) mozzarella, the *fior di latte* (flower of the milk), is made from the milk of the water buffalo, which were introduced to southern Italy in the sixteenth century. Unlike ordinary mozzarella cheese that you can buy almost anywhere, *mozzarella di bufala*, which is available in specialty shops, has a soft, uncommonly creamy texture and an almost sweet aroma. When you cut into it, it should drip with its own buttermilk. Buffalo milk mozzarella imported from Venezuela is now becoming available and is often comparable in quality to the Italian variety. American-made buffalo milk mozzarella and plain fresh mozzarella are available by mail order from the Mozzarella Company in Dallas, Texas (214) 741-4072.

About Italian fontina: Fontina comes from Italy's smallest region, the Valle d'Aosta, which shares its borders with France and Switzerland. It is a semi-soft cheese, made from unpasteurized cow's milk with 45 percent butterfat. With its mild and slightly nutty flavor, fontina is an excellent, creamy, melting cheese. Fontina has a soft, reddish brown rind that can be easily cut away.

Baked Pasta Tips

• Use a 9 × 13 × 3-inch glass, ceramic, or enamel-coated pan for preparing lasagna and cannelloni dishes. You can also use heavy-duty aluminum foil pans. They are great for transporting and convenient for cleanup, but aren't "dressy" enough for a more formal dinner.

• Coat the pan with some of the sauce—béchamel or tomato—before layering in the lasagna or cannelloni noodles because they tend to dry out on the bottom and become tough. Don't grease the pans with vegetable sprays, oil, or butter; this causes the pasta to brown and become crisp on the bottom.

• For the best results, don't make more than three layers in a lasagna. The lasagna won't bake in the prescribed time and will take on a heavy, less delicate quality.

• To grate some of the softer cheeses, grate them cold from the refrigerator; use a standard four-sided grater; and gently press on the cheese while sliding it across the large-hole grater.

• Fillings for cannelloni and ravioli can be prepared in advance and refrigerated for up to three days.

• Be careful not to overcook your baked pasta dishes. The sauces will dry out; the vegetables will be overcooked; and the pasta itself will turn rubbery. Because all the ingredients—except the cheeses—are already cooked in baked pasta dishes, you are basically heating the dish thoroughly and melting the cheeses, which blends and bonds the ingredients.

• For the best results when reheating baked pasta, reheat individual portions covered with microwave-safe wrap or waxed paper in the microwave oven for under a minute so as not to dry out the pasta.

• You can freeze baked pasta dishes. It's best to freeze them before baking; defrost in the refrigerator; and allow them to come to room temperature before baking.

▦ BÉCHAMEL SAUCE

1½ CUPS

Béchamel, *balsamella* in Italian, is a creamy white sauce that is an essential ingredient in most recipes for lasagna, cannelloni, and baked pasta dishes in general. The Italian version is similar to the classic French béchamel but is prepared somewhat differently — and I think more easily — and tends to be lighter. I like to use low-fat 1 percent milk, which makes the sauce particularly light, but you can use whole milk for a richer, creamier taste. For an even richer taste, add a tablespoon of mascarpone cheese to the finished sauce. Or for a lighter sauce, use skim milk as I recommend in Lean Lasagna (see pages 254–57).

At the restaurant and inn Al Sole in Maleo in Lombardy, the *balsamella* is prepared with a bit of finely chopped red onion or shallot. It gives the sauce a delicious flavor and masks the milky taste, which can sometimes be overpowering in a light vegetable dish. I liked the taste so much that I incorporated it into my recipe. Purists can omit it if they want. You can prepare béchamel in advance and keep it for up to 2 days in the refrigerator. Reheat in a microwave or double boiler before using.

1½ cups milk
3 tablespoons unsalted butter
2 tablespoons finely chopped red onion or shallots
2 tablespoons all-purpose flour
Pinch of salt

Scald the milk (heat it just to the point of boiling) either in a heat-proof glass measuring cup in a microwave oven or in a heavy saucepan on top of the stove, being careful not to boil it. Remove from the heat.

In a small saucepan, preferably one with a nonstick surface, heat the butter over medium-high heat until melted and bubbling. Add the red onion. Cook, stirring, until onion begins to soften, 2 to 3 minutes. Add the flour and salt. Using a small wire whisk, stir to combine with the butter and onion. Cook for 1 to 2 minutes. Turn off the heat.

Begin to add the milk to the butter and flour mixture a few tablespoons at a time, stirring well with the whisk after each addition. The mixture will seize up and become very thick at first, but as you add more milk and stir the mixture, it regains its liquidity. After you've added about a cup of the milk, the mixture will be fluid. Add all the remaining milk and stir well with the whisk. Turn the heat to medium. Cook, stirring, until the mixture is the consistency of heavy cream. Remove from the heat and use right away, or pour the sauce into a heat-proof glass measuring cup and cover securely with plastic wrap until ready to use. As the sauce stands exposed to the air, a skin will form on the top. Plastic wrap helps to prevent the skin from forming.

⊞ LASAGNA OF PAN-ROASTED EGGPLANT, MOZZARELLA, AND FRESH TOMATO SAUCE

6 SERVINGS

If you make only one lasagna in this book, this should be it. Inspired by the classic meat dish from northern Italy, the eggplant stands in for the meat in this creamy but hearty lasagna with a wonderfully robust flavor.

1 large eggplant (about 1½ pounds), stem end cut off and
  discarded and cut into 1-inch cubes
1 tablespoon kosher salt, plus extra for sprinkling on eggplant
¼ cup olive oil
1 clove garlic, pressed or finely minced
About ½ pound dry lasagna noodles (enough to make 3 layers)
1 recipe Béchamel Sauce (see pages 182–83)
3 cups Fresh Tomato Sauce (see page 86) or other tomato sauce
½ pound mozzarella cheese, shredded
⅓ cup freshly grated Parmesan cheese

Place the eggplant cubes in a large colander; sprinkle liberally with salt. Allow to stand and drain at least 30 minutes.

Heat the olive oil in a large skillet, preferably one with a non-stick surface, over medium-high heat. Add the eggplant. Cook, stirring frequently, until the eggplant is tender and just beginning to turn golden brown, 10 to 12 minutes. Add the garlic and cook 1 minute longer. Turn off the heat; set aside.

Bring a large pot of water to a rolling boil over high heat. Add the tablespoon of salt and the lasagna noodles. Cook, stirring occasionally, until the pasta is tender but firm, *al dente*, 5 to 7 minutes (depending on the type of pasta you are using). Drain; rinse pasta under cold water. Separate the noodles so they don't stick together.

Preheat the oven to 350°F. Prepare the béchamel sauce and spoon a few tablespoons into the bottom of a 9 × 13 × 3-inch glass, ceramic, or enamel-coated baking dish to coat it. Cover the bottom of the dish with a layer of lasagna noodles. They can overlap, but shouldn't come up the sides of the dish. Trim them with a knife to fit. Distribute half the eggplant evenly over the pasta. Pour 1 cup of the tomato sauce over the eggplant and use a rubber spatula to spread it evenly. Pour $1/2$ cup of the béchamel sauce over the tomato sauce so it is distributed evenly. Cover with a layer of the grated mozzarella (you should use about a third) and a sprinkling of Parmesan. Repeat with another layer of lasagna noodles, the remaining eggplant, 1 cup of tomato sauce, $1/2$ cup béchamel sauce, a third of the mozzarella cheese, and a sprinkling of Parmesan. Finish the lasagna with a layer of noodles and the remaining tomato sauce and béchamel sauce. Top with the remaining mozzarella and Parmesan.

Cover the dish securely with aluminum foil. (You can prepare this recipe ahead and refrigerate for up to a day; allow to come to room temperature before baking.) Bake on the topmost oven rack for 45 minutes. Remove the foil and continue baking until the top is just beginning to brown, about 15 minutes longer. Allow the lasagna to stand for 5 minutes before serving.

GREEN AND WHITE LASAGNA PRIMAVERA WITH BROCCOLI, ZUCCHINI, AND ASPARAGUS

6 SERVINGS

A combination of fresh green vegetables and mushrooms, a creamy white béchamel sauce, and lots of cheese make this lasagna deliciously rich, but fresh tasting. You can vary the vegetables to your own taste, but keep the quantity of vegetables approximately the same.

1 small bunch broccoli, heavy stems discarded and tops
    cut into small florets (to yield about 3 cups)
$1/2$ pound zucchini, ends discarded, cut in half lengthwise,
    and cut crosswise into $1/2$-inch-thick slices
6 asparagus spears, tough bottoms discarded and spears cut
    into 3 or 4 pieces
$1/4$ cup olive oil
$1/4$ pound mushrooms (preferably shiitake or crimini), stemmed,
    and caps thinly sliced
1 tablespoon kosher salt, plus extra for seasoning
Freshly ground black pepper
2 medium-size leeks (white part only), cut in half lengthwise,
    rinsed well between the layers to remove any sand or dirt,
    and cut crosswise into $1/2$-inch-thick slices
1 clove garlic, pressed or finely minced
About $1/2$ pound dry lasagna noodles (enough to make 3 layers)
1 recipe Béchamel Sauce (see page 182–83)
8 ounces Italian fontina cheese, rind removed and coarsely grated
$1/2$ cup freshly grated Parmesan cheese

Bring a small saucepan of water to boil over high heat. When the water boils, drop in the broccoli; cook exactly 3 minutes. Remove the broccoli with a slotted spoon and transfer to a colander. Rinse under cold water; drain. Drop the zucchini slices into the boiling water; cook exactly 1 minute. Remove the zucchini with a slotted spoon and transfer to a colander. Rinse under cold water; drain. Drop the asparagus into the boiling water; cook exactly 1 minute. Drain; rinse under cold water. Set the vegetables aside.

In a small skillet, heat 1 tablespoon of the oil over medium heat. Add the mushrooms and season with salt and pepper to taste. Cook, stirring gently, until tender, about 7 minutes. Turn off the heat; set aside.

In a large skillet, heat the remaining olive oil over medium heat. Add the leeks and season with salt to taste. Cook, stirring occasionally, until they are tender but not brown, 7 to 10 minutes. Add the garlic. Cook, stirring, 1 minute longer. Turn off the heat. Add the broccoli, zucchini, asparagus, and mushrooms to the leeks; stir to combine. Set aside.

Preheat the oven to 450°F. Bring a large pot of water to a rolling boil over high heat. Add the tablespoon of salt and the lasagna noodles. Cook, stirring occasionally, until the pasta is tender but firm, *al dente*, 5 to 7 minutes (depending on the type of pasta you are using). Drain; rinse pasta under cold water. Separate the noodles so they don't stick together.

Prepare the béchamel sauce and spread a few tablespoons over the bottom of a 9 × 13 × 3-inch glass, ceramic, or enamel-coated baking dish to coat it. Cover the bottom of the dish with a layer of lasagna noodles. The noodles can overlap, but they shouldn't come up the sides of the dish. Trim them with a knife to fit. Spread half the vegetable mixture over the pasta in an even layer. Pour ¹/₂ cup of the béchamel sauce over the vegetables so it is distributed evenly. Cover the vegetables with a layer of the grated fontina (use a little more than a third) and a sprinkling of the Parmesan. Repeat with another layer of lasagna noodles, vegetables, béchamel sauce, and the cheeses. Finish the lasagna with a layer of noodles, the remaining béchamel sauce, fontina, and a sprinkling of Parmesan.

Cover the dish securely with aluminum foil. (You can prepare this recipe ahead and refrigerate for up to a day; allow to come to room temperature before baking.) Bake on the topmost oven rack for 30 minutes. Remove the foil and continue baking until the top is brown, about 10 minutes longer. Allow the lasagna to stand for 5 minutes before serving.

AUTUMN LASAGNA WITH BUTTERNUT SQUASH, MUSHROOMS, AND ROASTED CHESTNUTS

6 SERVINGS

The best of fall's hearty harvest flavors blend with the robust taste of rich fontina and gorgonzola cheeses in this lasagna. Buy already peeled, ready-to-use butternut squash if you can find it fresh in your supermarket produce department. And if they're available, use wild mushroom varieties such as portobello, crimini, or shiitake to give an even more earthy taste to this dish.

1 medium-size eggplant (about 1½ pounds), stem end discarded and cut into 1-inch cubes (to yield 4 to 5 cups)
1 tablespoon kosher salt, plus extra for sprinkling on eggplant and seasoning

$^1/_4$ pound butternut squash, peeled, seeded, and cut into small dice
   (to yield about 2 cups)
$^1/_4$ cup olive oil
$^1/_2$ pound mushrooms, stemmed, caps thinly sliced
Freshly ground black pepper
1 clove garlic, pressed or finely minced
6 fresh chestnuts in their shells
About $^1/_2$ pound dry lasagna noodles (enough for 3 layers)
1 recipe Béchamel Sauce (see pages 182–83)
8 ounces Italian fontina cheese, rind removed and coarsely grated
$^1/_2$ cup freshly grated Parmesan cheese
3 ounces gorgonzola cheese, cut into small pieces

Place the eggplant cubes in a large colander; sprinkle liberally with salt. Allow to drain at least 30 minutes. Meanwhile, bring a small saucepan of water to boil over high heat. Drop in the squash and cook exactly 5 minutes. Drain; rinse in cold water and set aside.

Heat 1 tablespoon of the olive oil in a small skillet over medium heat. Add the mushrooms and season with salt and pepper to taste. Cook, stirring gently until tender, about 7 minutes. Set aside. Heat the remaining oil in a large skillet over medium-high heat. Add the eggplant. Cook, stirring, until the eggplant is tender and just beginning to turn brown, 10 to 12 minutes. Add the garlic and cook 1 minute longer. Add the mushrooms and squash; stir to combine. Turn off the heat and set aside.

Preheat the oven to 450°F. Use a sharp paring knife to cut an X on the tops of the chestnuts. Place them on a baking sheet; bake until the shells curl open and the chestnuts are tender, about 10 minutes. Allow to cool slightly. Peel away the shells with your fingers and thinly slice the chestnuts.

Bring a large pot of water to a rolling boil over high heat. Add the tablespoon of salt and the lasagna noodles. Cook, stirring occasionally, until the pasta is tender but firm, *al dente*, 5 to 7 minutes (depending on the type of pasta you are using). Drain; rinse pasta under cold water. Separate the noodles so they don't stick to-gether.

Prepare the béchamel sauce and spread a few tablespoons over the bottom of a 9 × 13 × 3-inch glass, ceramic, or enamel-coated baking dish to coat it. Cover the bottom of the dish with a layer of lasagna noodles. The noodles can overlap, but they shouldn't come up the sides of the dish. Trim them with a knife to fit. Spread half the vegetable mixture over the pasta in an even layer. Pour ½ cup of the béchamel sauce over the vegetables so it is distributed evenly. Sprinkle half the sliced chestnuts over the top. Cover the vegetables with a layer of the grated fontina (use about a third) and a sprinkling of Parmesan. Repeat with another layer of lasagna noodles, vegetables, chestnuts, béchamel sauce, and cheeses. Finish the lasagna with a layer of noodles, the remaining béchamel sauce and fontina cheese, and a sprinkling of Parmesan. Distribute the gorgonzola over the top.

Cover the dish securely with aluminum foil. (You can prepare this recipe ahead and refrigerate for up to a day; allow to come to room temperature before baking.) Bake on the topmost oven rack for 30 minutes. Remove the foil and continue baking until the top is brown, about 10 minutes longer. Allow the lasagna to stand for 5 minutes before serving.

RADICCHIO LASAGNA

6 SERVINGS

This recipe comes from Franco Colombani, the owner of the inn and restaurant Albergo del Sole in Maleo, Lombardy, in Italy. He calls it a *pasticcio*, which in Italian means pie. He makes this dish with layers of fresh pasta and lots of Swiss emmenthaler cheese, which I was surprised to discover because Lombardy produces so many wonderful cheeses. But it works perfectly in this recipe — the slight sweetness and nutty taste of the cheese balances the bitterness of the radicchio. One change I've made: Sr. Colombani sautés his radicchio in butter and *pancetta*, Italian bacon, which gives the finished dish a distinctive flavor. I've eliminated the *pancetta* to make this a meatless dish, but you can add a small piece (3 ounces) to the butter if you like. (Salt pork would be a substitute for pancetta.)

1 pound radicchio (1 to 2 small heads)
3 tablespoons unsalted butter or olive oil
1 clove garlic, pressed or finely minced
1 tablespoon kosher salt, plus extra for seasoning
About ½ pound dry lasagna noodles (enough to make 3 layers)
1 recipe Béchamel Sauce (see pages 182–83)
6 ounces Swiss emmenthaler cheese, coarsely grated
½ cup freshly grated Parmesan cheese

Cut the heads of radicchio into quarters and finely shred each section. You should have about 6 cups shredded radicchio. Melt the butter in a medium-size skillet over medium heat. Add the garlic and radicchio; season with salt to taste. Cook, stirring occasionally, until the radicchio is tender and the white parts have turned a brownish color and the red has turned a deep purple, 10 to 12 minutes. Turn off the heat and set aside.

Bring a large pot of water to a rolling boil over high heat. Add the tablespoon of salt and the lasagna noodles. Cook, stirring occasionally, until the pasta is tender but firm, *al dente*, 5 to 7 minutes (depending on the type of pasta you are using). Drain; rinse pasta under cold water. Separate the noodles so they don't stick together.

Preheat the oven to 350°F. Prepare the béchamel sauce and spread a few tablespoons over the bottom of the 9 × 13 × 3-inch glass, ceramic, or enamel-coated baking dish to coat it. Cover the bottom of the dish with a layer of lasagna noodles. They can overlap, but shouldn't come up the sides of the dish. Trim them with a knife to fit. Spread half the radicchio over the pasta in an even layer. Pour about ½ cup of the béchamel sauce over the radicchio so it is distributed evenly. Cover with a layer of the grated emmenthaler (use about a third) and a sprinkling of Parmesan. Repeat with another layer of lasagna noodles, radicchio, béchamel sauce, and the cheeses. Finish the lasagna with a layer of noodles, the remaining béchamel sauce, emmenthaler, and a sprinkling of Parmesan.

Cover the dish securely with aluminum foil. (You can prepare this recipe ahead and refrigerate for up to a day; allow to come to room temperature before baking.) Bake on the topmost oven rack for 30 minutes. Remove the foil and continue baking until the top is brown, about 10 minutes longer. Allow the lasagna to stand for 5 minutes before serving.

LASAGNA OF SPINACH AND BROCCOLI RABE

6 SERVINGS

The sharp, fresh taste of the spinach and broccoli is a delicious contrast to the rich creaminess of the cheeses and béchamel sauce in this lasagna. Be extra careful not to overbake this dish so the spinach and broccoli remain bright green and fresh tasting.

1 cup broccoli rabe florets, cut from 1 bunch broccoli rabe, stalks
    and leaves discarded (or use ordinary broccoli)
3 tablespoons olive oil
1 10-ounce package fresh spinach, stems removed, leaves rinsed
    in cold water to remove any sand or dirt, and spun dry
1 clove garlic, pressed or finely minced
1 tablespoon kosher salt, plus extra for seasoning
$1/3$ cup pine nuts
About $1/2$ pound dry lasagna noodles (enough to make 3 layers)
1 recipe Béchamel Sauce (see pages 182–83)
8 ounces Italian fontina cheese, rind removed and coarsely grated
$1/2$ cup freshly grated Parmesan cheese

Bring a small saucepan of water to boil over high heat. When the water boils, drop in the broccoli florets and cook exactly 1 minute. Drain in a colander. Rinse under cold water and drain.

Heat the oil in a large skillet over medium-high heat. Add the spinach and garlic; season with salt to taste. Cook, stirring until the spinach is tender and the water in the pan has cooked away, 3 to 5 minutes. Add the blanched broccoli florets and stir to combine. Set aside.

Place a small skillet over medium heat. Add the pine nuts. Cook, stirring constantly and watching closely, until they are toasted and light golden brown, about 5 minutes. Turn off the heat and set aside. (Be careful with the pine nuts, they will quickly burn if left unattended.)

Bring a large pot of water to a rolling boil over high heat. Add the tablespoon of salt and the lasagna noodles. Cook, stirring occasionally, until the pasta is tender but firm, *al dente*, 5 to 7 minutes (depending on the type of pasta you are using). Drain; rinse pasta under cold water. Separate the noodles so they don't stick together.

Preheat the oven to 350°F. Prepare the béchamel sauce and spread a few tablespoons over the bottom of a 9 × 13 × 3-inch glass, ceramic, or enamel-coated baking dish to coat it. Cover the bottom of the dish with a layer of lasagna noodles. The noodles can overlap, but shouldn't come up the sides of the dish. Trim them with a knife to fit. Spread half the spinach and broccoli mixture over the pasta in an even layer, making sure the pasta is mostly covered. Pour ½ cup of the béchamel sauce over the spinach and broccoli so it is distributed evenly. Cover with a layer of the grated fontina (use about a third), a sprinkling of the Parmesan, and half the pine nuts. Repeat with another layer of lasagna noodles, spinach and broccoli, béchamel sauce, cheeses, and the remaining pine nuts. Finish the lasagna with a layer of noodles, the remaining béchamel sauce and fontina, and a sprinkling of Parmesan.

Cover the dish securely with aluminum foil. (You can prepare this recipe ahead and refrigerate for up to a day; allow to come to room temperature before baking.) Bake on the topmost oven rack for 30 minutes. Remove the foil and continue baking until the top is just beginning to brown, about 10 minutes longer. Allow the lasagna to stand for 5 minutes before serving.

▨ ARTICHOKE LASAGNA

6 SERVINGS

This dish was inspired by one of my favorite recipes, Marcella Hazan's *torta di carciofi*. I loved the taste of the artichokes and cheeses baked in a crust, so I knew artichokes would be delicious baked in pasta.

When trimming the artichokes, be careful to remove all the tough outer leaves, otherwise, you'll find inedible fibrous shreds of artichoke in the lasagna. And be careful not to overbake this lasagna or it will become dry and less flavorful.

4 medium-size artichokes (about 2 pounds)
3 tablespoons olive oil
1 clove garlic, pressed or finely minced
1 cup water
1 tablespoon kosher salt
About $\frac{1}{2}$ pound dry lasagna noodles (enough to make 3 layers)
1 recipe Béchamel Sauce (see pages 182–83)
8 ounces Italian fontina cheese, rind removed and coarsely grated
$\frac{1}{2}$ cup freshly grated Parmesan cheese

For each artichoke, peel away the tough dark green leaves. Starting with the leaves closest to the stem, break off the leaves all around the artichoke until only the yellow-green leaves are visible. Do not use scissors or a knife for this, the leaves will break naturally at the point where the tough part ends and the tender part begins. Use a serrated knife to cut 1 to 2 inches off the top of the artichoke, use a small paring knife to peel the stem, and trim around the base. Cut the artichoke into quarters lengthwise. Cut out the choke and the spiny leaves about it. Slice the artichokes lengthwise as thinly as possible.

Heat the oil in a large skillet over medium heat. Add the garlic and artichokes. Cook, stirring, about 3 minutes. Add the water and bring to a boil. Cover the pan; reduce the heat to medium-low. Simmer until the artichokes are tender and the water has mostly cooked away, about 20 minutes. If water is still in the pan, continue cooking the artichokes, uncovered, until the water is evaporated, 3 to 5 minutes longer. Set aside.

Bring a large pot of water to a rolling boil over high heat. Add the tablespoon of salt and the lasagna noodles. Cook, stirring occasionally, until the pasta is tender but firm, *al dente*, 5 to 7 minutes (depending on the type of pasta you are using). Drain; rinse pasta under cold water. Separate the noodles so they don't stick together.

Preheat the oven to 350°F. Prepare the béchamel sauce and spread a few tablespoons over the bottom of a 9 × 13 × 3-inch

glass, ceramic, or enamel-coated baking dish to coat it. Cover the bottom of the dish with a layer of lasagna noodles. They can overlap, but shouldn't come up the sides of the dish. Trim them with a knife to fit. Spread half the artichokes over the pasta in an even layer, making sure that the pasta is mostly covered. Pour about $1/2$ cup of the béchamel sauce over the artichokes so it is distributed evenly. Cover with a layer of the grated fontina (use about a third) and a sprinkling of Parmesan. Repeat with another layer of lasagna noodles, artichokes, béchamel sauce, and the cheeses. Finish the lasagna with a layer of noodles, the remaining béchamel sauce and fontina, and a sprinkling of Parmesan.

Cover the dish securely with aluminum foil. (You can prepare this recipe ahead and refrigerate for up to a day; allow to come to room temperature before baking.) Bake on the topmost oven rack for 30 minutes. Remove the foil and continue baking until the top is just beginning to brown, 5 to 7 minutes longer. Allow the lasagna to stand for 5 minutes before serving.

LASAGNA WITH ZUCCHINI, SUMMER SQUASH, BROCCOLI, AND SHIITAKE MUSHROOMS

6 SERVINGS

A colorful, light and fresh-tasting lasagna.

4 tablespoons olive oil
1 large Bermuda or other sweet onion, peeled, cut in half and
    thinly sliced
1 clove garlic, pressed or finely minced
$\frac{1}{2}$ pound zucchini, ends discarded and cut into 2-inch julienne
    strips
$\frac{1}{2}$ pound summer squash, ends discarded and cut into
    2-inch julienne strips
1 tablespoon kosher salt, plus extra for seasoning
$\frac{1}{4}$ pound shiitake mushrooms, stemmed, and caps thinly sliced
2 cups broccoli florets
About $\frac{1}{2}$ pound dry lasagna noodles (enough to make 3 layers)
1 recipe Béchamel Sauce (see pages 182–83)
8 ounces Italian fontina cheese, rind removed and coarsely grated
Freshly grated Parmesan cheese

Heat 2 tablespoons of the oil in a large skillet over medium-high heat. Add the onion and garlic. Cook, stirring, until the onion begins to soften, about 2 to 3 minutes. Add the zucchini and summer squash; season with salt to taste. Cook until the zucchini and squash are tender, about 5 minutes longer. Remove from the heat.

In a separate small skillet, heat the remaining oil over medium-high heat. Add the mushrooms and season with salt to taste. Cook, stirring until the mushrooms are tender, about 7 minutes. Transfer to the skillet with the onion and zucchini.

Meanwhile, bring a small saucepan of water to boil over high heat. Add the broccoli and cook 1 minute. Drain; rinse broccoli under cold water. Add the broccoli to the pan with the other vegetables; stir to combine. Set aside.

Bring a large pot of water to a rolling boil over high heat. Add the tablespoon of salt and the lasagna noodles. Cook, stirring occasionally, until the pasta is tender but firm, *al dente*, 5 to 7 minutes (depending on the type of pasta you are using). Drain; rinse pasta under cold water. Separate the noodles so they don't stick together.

Preheat the oven to 350°F. Prepare the béchamel sauce and spread a few tablespoons over the bottom of a 9 × 13 × 3-inch glass, ceramic, or enamel-coated baking dish to coat it. Cover the bottom of the dish with a layer of lasagna noodles. They can overlap, but shouldn't come up the sides of the dish. Trim them with a knife to fit. Spread half the vegetable mixture over the pasta in an even layer, making sure that the pasta is mostly covered. Pour about ½ cup of the béchamel sauce over the vegetables so it is distributed evenly. Cover with a layer of the grated fontina (use about a third) and a sprinkling of Parmesan. Repeat with another layer of lasagna noodles, vegetables, béchamel sauce, and the cheeses. Finish the lasagna with a layer of noodles, the remaining béchamel sauce and fontina, and a sprinkling of Parmesan.

Cover the dish securely with aluminum foil. (You can prepare this recipe ahead and refrigerate for up to a day; allow to come to room temperature before baking.) Bake on the topmost oven rack for 30 minutes. Remove the foil and continue baking until the top is just beginning to brown, about 10 minutes longer. Allow the lasagna to stand for 5 minutes before serving.

LASAGNA WITH QUICK MUSHROOM RAGÙ

6 SERVINGS

This easy lasagna can be prepared with any fresh or store-bought tomato sauce that's been combined with sautéed mushrooms. With a variety of mushrooms and good-melting cheeses, the finished dish has a delicious intensity of flavor.

1 recipe Quick Mushroom Ragù (see page 105)
1 tablespoon kosher salt
About ½ pound dry lasagna noodles (enough to make 3 layers)
1 recipe Béchamel Sauce (see pages 182–83)
4 ounces Italian fontina cheese, rind removed and coarsely grated
2 ounces Swiss emmenthaler cheese, coarsely grated
2 ounces mozzarella cheese, coarsely grated
½ cup freshly grated Parmesan cheese

Prepare the Quick Mushroom Ragù and set aside.

Bring a large pot of water to a rolling boil over high heat. Add the salt and lasagna noodles. Cook, stirring occasionally, until the pasta is tender but firm, *al dente*, 5 to 7 minutes (depending on the type of pasta you are using). Drain; rinse pasta under cold water. Separate the noodles so they don't stick together.

Preheat the oven to 350°F. Prepare the béchamel sauce and spread a few tablespoons over the bottom of a 9 × 13 × 3-inch glass, ceramic, or enamel-coated baking dish to coat it. Cover the bottom of the dish with a layer of lasagna noodles. They can over-lap, but shouldn't come up the sides of the dish. Trim them with a knife to fit. Spread a third of the mushroom ragù over the pasta in an even layer, making sure the pasta is completely covered.

Pour about ½ cup of the béchamel sauce over the ragù so it is distributed evenly. Cover with a layer of the grated cheeses (use about a third) and a sprinkling of Parmesan. Repeat with another layer of lasagna noodles, ragù, béchamel sauce, and the cheeses. Finish the lasagna with a layer of noodles, the remaining ragù, béchamel sauce, and cheeses.

Cover the dish securely with aluminum foil. (You can prepare this recipe ahead and refrigerate for up to a day; allow to come to room temperature before baking.) Bake on the topmost oven rack for 30 minutes. Remove the foil and continue baking until the top is just beginning to brown, about 10 minutes longer. Allow the lasagna to stand for 5 minutes before serving.

SOUTHERN ITALIAN-STYLE LASAGNA WITH SPINACH PASTA

6 SERVINGS

Many layers of fresh pasta transform this simple dish into something extraordinary.

1 tablespoon kosher salt, plus extra for seasoning
1 pound fresh spinach pasta (see page 11), cut into 4 × 9-inch
   strips
1 pound whole-milk ricotta cheese
¼ cup mascarpone cheese
Freshly ground black pepper
½ cup freshly grated Parmesan cheese, plus a few extra
   tablespoons
3 cups Fresh Tomato Sauce (see page 86)
1 pound whole-milk mozzarella cheese, coarsely grated

Make a lasagne

ling boil over high heat. Add the
a noodles. Cook, stirring occa-
ut firm, *al dente*, about 5 minutes.

parate the noodles so they don't

cotta, mascarpone, salt and pep-
mesan; beat briskly with a wire

read a few tablespoons of the
9 × 13 × 3-inch glass, ceramic,
at it.

Arr ngle layer in the baking dish to
complet pasta noodles can overlap, but
they should not come up the sides of the dish. Trim the ends with a
sharp knife or kitchen shears to fit. Spoon about $^3/_4$ cup of the
tomato sauce over the pasta; cover with another layer of pasta.
Spread a third of the ricotta mixture over the pasta with a rubber
spatula or wooden spoon; cover with another layer of pasta. Distribute about a third of the mozzarella over the pasta; cover with
another layer of pasta. Repeat the layers two more times in the following order: tomato sauce/pasta; ricotta cheese mixture/pasta;
mozzarella/pasta. Cover the top layer of pasta with the remaining tomato sauce and Parmesan. About 1 inch of space should be
between the edge of the dish and the top of the lasagna.

Cover the dish securely with aluminum foil. (You can prepare
this recipe ahead and refrigerate for up to a day; allow to come to
room temperature before baking.) Bake on the topmost oven rack
for 45 minutes. Remove the foil and continue baking until the top
is just beginning to brown, about 10 minutes longer. Allow the
lasagna to stand for 5 minutes before serving.

CANNELLONI FILLED WITH WILD MUSHROOMS AND MASCARPONE

6 SERVINGS

In southern Italy, cannelloni are usually made with sheets of fresh pasta dough. For convenience, I like to use the Italian dry pasta sheets (made by Delverde) now available in some supermarkets and Italian specialty food shops. You can also use lasagna noodles and preformed cannelloni pasta tubes.

3 tablespoons olive oil
1 pound fresh wild mushrooms (portobello, shiitake or crimini),
    stemmed, and caps thinly sliced
1 tablespoon kosher salt, plus extra for seasoning
Freshly ground black pepper
1 clove garlic, pressed or finely minced
2 tablespoons finely chopped fresh parsley
2 tablespoons mascarpone cheese
6 sheets precooked lasagna or 12 cannelloni tubes
1 recipe Béchamel Sauce (see pages 182–83)
$^1/_3$ cup freshly grated Parmesan cheese

Heat the oil in a large skillet over medium-high heat. Add the mushrooms; season with salt and pepper to taste. Cook, stirring, until the mushrooms are tender, 7 to 10 minutes. Add the garlic and cook 1 minute longer. Turn off the heat. Stir in the parsley and mascarpone. Set aside.

Bring a large pot of water to a rolling boil over high heat. Add the tablespoon of salt and the pasta. Cook, stirring occasionally, until the pasta is tender, about 5 minutes. (If you are using preformed cannelloni pasta, cook until tender, about 10 minutes.)

Drain; rinse pasta under cold water. Separate the noodles so they don't stick together. If you are using the lasagna sheets, cut them in half to make 12 pieces.

Preheat the oven to 350°F. Prepare the béchamel sauce and spread a few tablespoons over the bottom of a 9 × 13 × 3-inch glass, ceramic, or enamel-coated baking dish to coat it. If you are using pasta sheets, place a piece of the pasta on a clean work surface in front of you. Place a heaping teaspoonful of the mushroom mixture at one end of the pasta strip, about 1 inch from the end. Roll to make a cannelloni tube (1 to 2 inches in diameter.) Place the rolled, filled, cannelloni in the baking dish. Repeat until all the filling and all the pasta have been rolled up, gauging as you go to make them come out evenly and placing the cannelloni closely together in the dish. (If you are using preformed cannelloni pasta, fill each tube with some of the mushroom mixture and place in the baking dish.)

Pour the remaining béchamel sauce over the cannelloni in the baking dish. Sprinkle the Parmesan over the top. Cover the baking dish securely with aluminum foil. Place in the oven and bake until the sauce is bubbling and the cheese is melted on top, about 30 minutes. Allow to stand, uncovered, 5 minutes before serving.

▣ CANNELLONI OF ZUCCHINI AND SUMMER SQUASH, RICOTTA, AND FRESH BASIL

6 SERVINGS

The green zucchini and yellow summer squash make a colorful and delicious filling for cannelloni when combined with ricotta and fresh basil. Because most of the ricotta cheese you can buy in supermarkets is lighter and less flavorful than the ricotta you find in Italy, adding some mascarpone to the ricotta improves the taste and texture. You can omit it for a leaner dish.

2 tablespoons olive oil

½ pound zucchini, ends discarded and cut into julienne strips

½ pound summer squash, ends discarded and cut into julienne strips

1 tablespoon kosher salt, plus extra for seasoning

¼ cup chopped fresh basil leaves

½ cup whole-milk ricotta cheese

2 tablespoons mascarpone cheese

6 sheets lasagna or 12 cannelloni tubes

2 cups Fresh Tomato Sauce (see page 86)

⅓ cup freshly grated Parmesan cheese plus more for serving

Heat the oil in a medium-size skillet over medium heat. Add the zucchini and yellow squash; season with salt to taste. Cook, stirring, until the squash are tender, about 5 minutes. Transfer to a small mixing bowl. Add the basil, ricotta, and mascarpone. Stir well to combine. Set aside.

Bring a large pot of water to a rolling boil over high heat. Add the tablespoon of salt and the pasta. Cook, stirring occasionally, until the pasta is soft and pliable, 3 to 5 minutes. (If you are using preformed cannelloni tubes, cook until tender, about 10 minutes.) Drain; rinse pasta under cold water. Separate the noodles so they don't stick together. If you are using the lasagna sheets, cut them in half to make 12 pieces.

Preheat the oven to 350°F. Spread a few tablespoons of the tomato sauce over the bottom of a 9 × 13 × 3-inch glass, ceramic, or enamel-coated baking dish to coat it. Working with one piece of pasta at a time, place a piece on a clean work surface in front of you. Place a heaping teaspoonful of the zucchini mixture at one end of the pasta strip, about 1 inch from the end. Roll to make a cannelloni tube 1 to 2 inches in diameter. Place the cannelloni in the baking dish. Repeat until all the filling and all the pasta have been rolled up, gauging as you go to make them come out evenly and placing the cannelloni as close together as possible in the dish. (If you are using preformed cannelloni pasta, fill each tube with some of the zucchini mixture and place in the baking dish.)

Pour the remaining tomato sauce over the cannelloni in the baking dish. Sprinkle the Parmesan over the tomato sauce. Cover the baking dish securely with aluminum foil. Place in the oven and bake until the sauce is bubbling, about 30 minutes. Serve with Parmesan.

CANNELLONI WITH CARAMELIZED LEEK AND ONION, ARUGULA, AND RICOTTA

6 SERVINGS

The arugula in this recipe adds a subtle sharp taste that perfectly contrasts with the sweetness of the caramelized leek-and-onion mixture.

3 tablespoons olive oil

1 medium-size leek (white part only), cut in half lengthwise, rinsed well between the layers to remove any sand or dirt, and thinly sliced

1 medium-size onion, peeled, cut in half and thinly sliced (to yield about 2 cups)

1 tablespoon kosher salt, plus extra for seasoning

1 small bunch arugula, stems cut off and discarded, leaves rinsed well in several changes of water and coarsely chopped

1/2 cup whole-milk ricotta cheese

2 tablespoons mascarpone cheese

6 sheets lasagna or 12 cannelloni tubes

2 cups Fresh Tomato Sauce (see page 86)

1/3 cup freshly grated Parmesan cheese, plus more for serving

Heat the oil in a large skillet over medium heat. Add the leek and onion; season with salt to taste. Cook, stirring occasionally, until the onion is deep golden brown but not burned, 35 to 40 minutes. Add the arugula and cook 3 to 5 minutes longer. Transfer to a small mixing bowl. Add the ricotta and mascarpone; stir well to combine. Set aside.

Bring a large pot of water to a rolling boil over high heat. Add the tablespoon of salt and the pasta. Cook, stirring occasionally, until the pasta is soft and pliable, 3 to 5 minutes. (If you are using preformed cannelloni pasta, cook until tender, about 10 minutes.) Drain; rinse pasta under cold water. Separate the noodles so they don't stick together. If you are using the lasagna sheets, cut them in half to make 12 pieces.

Preheat the oven to 350°F. Spread a few tablespoons of the tomato sauce over the bottom of a 9 × 13 × 3-inch glass, ceramic, or enamel-coated baking dish to coat it. Working with one piece of pasta at a time, place a piece on a clean work surface in front of you. Place a heaping teaspoonful of the leek, onion, and ricotta mixture at one end of the pasta strip, about 1 inch from the end. Roll to make a cannelloni tube about 1 inch in diameter. Place the cannelloni in the baking dish. Repeat until all the filling and all the pasta have been rolled up, gauging as you go to make them come out evenly and placing the cannelloni as close together as possible in the pan. (If you are using preformed cannelloni pasta, fill with leek, onion, and arugula mixture and place in the baking dish.)

Pour the remaining tomato sauce over the cannelloni in the baking dish. Sprinkle the Parmesan over the sauce. Cover the baking dish securely with aluminum foil. Place in the oven and bake until the sauce is bubbling, about 30 minutes. Serve with Parmesan.

SFORMATO OF PENNE WITH GORGONZOLA AND SPINACH

4 SERVINGS

Gorgonzola, named for the town where it was first produced north of Milan, is a strong-scented, flavorful cheese made from cow's milk. Originally, the moldy blue streaks in the cheese developed when fresh milk was added to old. Today, while gorgonzola is still aged in caves in the Alpine towns of Valsassina and Val Brembana, long copper pins are inserted into the cheeses to allow air in and the mold to form. The two types of gorgonzola are *naturale*, which is the more pungent and strongly flavored, and *dolcelatte*, which is less-aged and therefore milder and creamier. Most stores that carry Gorgonzola usually have the *dolce* because it appeals to a wider clientele. You can use either one in this recipe.

This is a fast and easy dish to prepare. Unmold the baked pasta onto a festive round platter decorated with arugula, it makes a stylish presentation for such a simple dish. Note that the pasta is undercooked when it is boiled. This means that it will not be overcooked after it is baked.

1 pound dry penne
2 cups chopped fresh spinach leaves that have been stemmed
    and rinsed well in several changes of cold water
1 tablespoon kosher salt
$^1/_2$ cups light cream or half-and-half
6 ounces Italian gorgonzola cheese, cut into small pieces
$^1/_4$ cup mascarpone cheese
Unsalted butter (for coating the baking dish)
Freshly grated Parmesan cheese

Preheat the oven to 450°F.

Bring a large pot of water to a rolling boil over high heat. Add the penne and salt. Cook, stirring occasionally, until the pasta is almost tender but still crunchy, about 5 minutes. Add the spinach and drain. Transfer to a large mixing bowl.

Meanwhile, heat the cream with the gorgonzola and mascarpone in a small saucepan over medium heat until the cheeses are melted and combined with the cream. Pour the gorgonzola sauce over the penne and spinach; mix well. Allow to cool to lukewarm. Stir again and transfer the penne and gorgonzola to a lightly buttered 6-quart soufflé dish or other round, deep baking dish. Cover with aluminum foil and bake 30 minutes. Remove from the oven and allow to stand 10 minutes. Remove the foil and run a knife around the inside of the baking dish. Place an inverted plate over the top of the baking dish and carefully turn the plate and baking dish over together so the plate is on the bottom. The molded pasta should come out easily. Serve at once with Parmesan cheese.

CAVATAPPI BAKED WITH SWEET ONIONS AND FONTINA

6 SERVINGS

The delicate, sweet flavor of this rich dish comes from the onions. If you can't find Italian fontina, use mozzarella, Asiago, or belpaese cheese. Cavatappi is corkscrew shaped pasta. You can substitute rotini, fusilli, or another squiggly pasta shape.

1/4 cup olive oil
3 large Vidalia onions (about 1 1/2 to 2 pounds), peeled and
    thinly sliced

Kosher salt

Freshly ground black pepper

1 pound dry cavatappi, fusilli, or rotini

4 ounces Italian fontina cheese, rind discarded and cut into
  ¹/₂-inch cubes

¹/₂ cup heavy cream

¹/₃ cup mascarpone cheese

¹/₂ cup freshly grated Parmesan cheese

Unsalted butter (for coating the baking dish)

Preheat the oven to 400°F. Heat the oil in a large skillet over medium-high heat. Add the onions; season with salt and pepper to taste. Cook, stirring frequently to prevent burning, until golden brown, about 25 minutes.

Meanwhile, bring a large pot of water to a rolling boil over high heat. Add the tablespoon of salt and the cavatappi. Cook, stirring frequently, until the pasta is tender but firm, *al dente*, 7 to 10 minutes. Drain; transfer to a large mixing bowl. Add the onions, fontina, cream, mascarpone, and Parmesan; mix well. Pour the pasta mixture into a buttered 9 × 13 × 3-inch glass, ceramic, or enamel-coated baking dish; spread into an even layer. Bake until the top is brown and bubbly, about 20 minutes. Allow to stand 5 minutes before serving.

⊞ BAKED CHEESE TORTELLINI WITH BROCCOLI AND FENNEL

4 SERVINGS

This is a quick and easy recipe that makes an impressive presentation. The combination of fennel and broccoli is one of my favorites. I generally wouldn't recommend tortellini sold in supermarkets, but in this recipe it will serve you well. Be careful not to overbake this dish because the broccoli will turn limp and lose a lot of flavor.

$1/2$ pound prepared fresh cheese tortellini (or use dry tortellini)
1 large fennel bulb, stalks and leaves discarded, bulb cut in
    half lengthwise, and sliced crosswise into $1/4$-inch strips
2 cups fresh broccoli florets (about $1/2$ a large bunch)
Unsalted butter (for coating the baking dish)
1 recipe Béchamel Sauce (see pages 182–83) prepared without
    red onion or shallots
4 ounces mozzarella cheese, grated
$1/3$ cup freshly grated Parmesan cheese

Bring a large saucepan of water to a rolling boil over high heat. Add the tortellini. After the water comes back to the boil, cook for 5 minutes. Drain; transfer to a large mixing bowl.

Bring another saucepan of water to a boil over high heat. Add the fennel and broccoli; cook for 1 minute. Drain; rinse under cold water. Add the fennel and broccoli to the tortellini; toss well to combine.

Preheat the oven to 350°F. Lightly butter a 9 × 3-inch oval or rectangular glass, ceramic, or enamel-coated baking dish. Spread the tortellini and vegetables in the dish evenly. Prepare the béchamel sauce; pour over the tortellini. Use a rubber spatula to distribute it evenly over the pasta and vegetables. Sprinkle the mozzarella over the béchamel; then the Parmesan over the top. Cover the dish securely with aluminum foil. Bake on the topmost oven rack for 10 minutes. Uncover and bake until the top is beginning to brown, about 10 minutes longer. Allow to stand 5 minutes before serving.

✳ BAKED ZITI WITH FONTINA CHEESE AND THREE KINDS OF SQUASH

6 SERVINGS

This version of macaroni and cheese will appeal to kids of all ages. The three kinds of squash lend a colorful accent to this rich and creamy dish.

1 pound dry ziti, penne, or macaroni
1 tablespoon kosher salt, plus extra for seasoning
6 tablespoons ($^3/_4$ stick) unsalted butter (plus some for coating
    the baking dish)
1 small onion, finely chopped
1 clove garlic, pressed or finely minced
1 medium-size zucchini, ends discarded and coarsely grated
    or cut into fine julienne strips
1 medium-size summer squash, ends discarded and coarsely
    grated or cut into fine julienne strips
1 cup peeled, seeded, and coarsely grated fresh pumpkin or
    Hubbard squash
3 tablespoons all-purpose flour
$1^1/_2$ cups hot milk
8 ounces Italian fontina cheese, rind removed and coarsely grated
Freshly grated Parmesan cheese

Preheat the oven to 350°F. Bring a large pot of water to a rolling boil over high heat. Add the ziti and the tablespoon of salt. Cook, stirring occasionally, until the pasta is crunchy, 5 minutes. Drain well; transfer to a large mixing bowl.

Melt 3 tablespoons of the butter in a large skillet over medium-high heat. Add the onion and garlic; cook, stirring, until the onion begins to soften, about 2 minutes. Add the zucchini, squash, and pumpkin; season with salt to taste. Lower the heat to medium and cook, stirring gently, until the pumpkin is tender, about 10 minutes. Add the vegetables to the pasta.

Melt the remaining butter in a small saucepan over medium-high heat. When the butter foams, add the flour and stir briskly with a wire whisk until it is completely incorporated into the butter. Do not let it brown. Remove from the heat. Add the milk $1/4$ cup at a time, beating with a wire whisk until each addition is absorbed. When all the milk has been added, return the pan to medium-low heat. Warm the sauce, stirring, until it thickens and is the consistency of heavy cream, about 5 minutes. Turn off the heat.

Add the white sauce along with the grated fontina to the pasta; toss well to combine. Pour the pasta and vegetable mixture into a lightly buttered, deep, 8-cup glass or ceramic baking dish, such as a soufflé dish; and top with the Parmesan. Bake until the top is brown and bubbly, about 50 minutes. Let stand a few minutes before serving.

✳ BAKED SHELLS WITH RADICCHIO AND FOUR CHEESES

6 SERVINGS

The combination of the soft shape of the shells and the ripples of red radicchio make for a sensational presentation.

1 pound dry small pasta shells
1 tablespoon kosher salt
1 small head radicchio (about ½ pound), shredded
2 cups light cream or half-and-half
4 ounces gorgonzola cheese, crumbled
4 ounces Asiago fresco or taleggio cheese, cut into small pieces
4 ounces Italian fontina cheese, rind removed and coarsely grated
Unsalted butter (for coating the baking dish)
⅓ cup freshly grated Parmesan cheese, plus extra for serving

Preheat the oven to 350°F. Bring a large pot of water to a rolling boil over high heat. Add the pasta and the tablespoon of salt. Cook, stirring occasionally, until the pasta is tender but firm, *al dente*, 7 to 10 minutes. Drain well; transfer to a large mixing bowl.

Add the radicchio, cream, and cheeses to the pasta; season with salt to taste. Toss well to combine. Transfer to a lightly buttered 9 × 3-inch oval baking dish. Cover with aluminum foil and bake for 45 minutes. Increase the oven temperature to 450°F. Uncover the pasta and bake until the top is brown, an additional 15 minutes. Let stand a few minutes before serving. Serve with grated Parmesan.

◪ LINGUINE BAKED WITH ZUCCHINI, TOMATOES, AND BASIL IN PARCHMENT

6 SERVINGS

Pasta baked in a parchment package, what the Italians call *al cartocchio*, makes a stunning presentation. You can do all the preparation in advance and pop the little packages into the oven at the last minute. You can substitute aluminum foil for the parchment paper, and other vegetables can be added to or used in place of the zucchini.

1 pound dry linguine

1 tablespoon kosher salt, plus extra for seasoning

1 pound zucchini, ends discarded and cut into julienne strips

3 plum tomatoes, peeled, seeded, and chopped

1 clove garlic, pressed or finely minced

12 tablespoons extra virgin olive oil

6 fresh basil leaves, cut into chiffonade strips

6 single sheets of parchment (or use double sheets of standard-
   width aluminum foil, 9 inches long)

Bring a large pot of water to a rolling boil over high heat. Add the linguine and the tablespoon of salt. Cook, stirring occasionally, 6 minutes (you want the pasta to be undercooked). Drain.

Preheat the oven to 350°F. Arrange the pasta in small, equal piles on the parchment or foil sheets. Top each portion of pasta with some of the zucchini, tomato, garlic, a sprinkling of salt, and two tablespoons olive oil. Seal the packets by folding the sheets in half over the pasta and zucchini and turning the edges over to crimp the sides. Place the packets on baking sheets and bake in the oven for 10 minutes. Place each packet on a serving plate, open them before serving, and garnish with some of the basil.

RAVIOLI AND FILLINGS

Homemade ravioli are among the most elegant and impressive of pasta dishes. With their irregular shapes and uncommon fillings, they are both intriguing and delicious. Eating ravioli is much like opening a present: you anticipate, and then enjoy the surprise hidden inside. Without a doubt, homemade ravioli surpasses any that you can buy.

The absolute best ravioli are prepared with your own homemade pasta dough (see the recipes on pages 8–10) rolled out as thinly as you or your machine can make it. The delicate egg-enriched sheets raise the ravioli to great heights, making them incomparably light and tender—and truly wonderful. But time being the precious commodity that it is, alternatives and shortcuts are necessary if you want ravioli to become part of your cooking repertoire.

In bigger cities, you can often buy prepared pasta in sheets that can be cut into squares or circles and filled for ravioli, although I have found that even very good store-bought fresh pasta sheets may require some additional rolling through the pasta machine rollers to make them delicately thin. While this is the best alternative to homemade pasta, it is not consistently and uniformly available even in major cities, let alone smaller towns. So you might consider another option for ravioli wrappers: oriental egg-pasta squares—called wonton or potsticker wrappers—sold in specialty food stores and some supermarkets. They produce a slightly less tender ravioli when cooked, but are still a good alternative to homemade fresh pasta.

Approximately 1 pound of pasta dough makes enough ravioli for six generous servings as a main course. The following filling recipes make approximately 1½ cups of filling, which should adequately fill 1 pound of pasta that's been cut into 2-inch circles, squares, or triangles for ravioli, but it's always difficult to make the pasta and filling come out even.

Sauce suggestions are given for each recipe, and some recipes for sauces are provided if they do not appear elsewhere in the book. Feel free to experiment with different sauces that you like or have on hand.

Ravioli Tips and General Filling and Cooking Instructions

• You can buy ravioli cutters in square or round shapes. These have serrated edges to make cutting the dough somewhat easy, and it gives the ravioli a decorative appearance.

• To make triangles and semi-circles, cut the sheets of dough into squares or circles, put some filling into the center of the square or circle of dough, and fold it in half to make triangular or semi-circular ravioli.

• Another option for shaping ravioli is to use a ravioli template. The template resembles a shallow egg crate: you lay one sheet of pasta over it, place a spoonful of filling in each indentation, place another pasta sheet on top, and use your rolling pin to seal and cut the ravioli.

• Fillings can usually be kept in the refrigerator for up to 3 days. I like to make the fillings one day and fill and cook the ravioli the next day. It makes the process easier.

• When filling ravioli, use no more than 1 teaspoon of filling per ravioli; less is better because the filling expands during cooking. Overfilling can result in the ravioli bursting during cooking.

• Before sealing the ravioli, use your fingers to press out any air pockets from around the filling.

• To seal the ravioli, lightly wet the edges of the dough with water so the sides adhere when pressed together. Use a knife or pastry cutter to trim the sealed edges.

• Store filled ravioli on a wire mesh drying rack (see the pasta primer on page 8) until ready to cook.

• Cook the ravioli in a large quantity of briskly boiling salted water, just as you would unfilled pasta. Cooking time is approximately the same as for other pasta, 7 to 10 minutes.

• Depending on the size of the ravioli, figure approximately 6 ravioli per person.

SPINACH, RICOTTA, AND CARAMELIZED ONION RAVIOLI

ABOUT 1½ CUPS

The caramelized onion is a delicious addition of flavor to this classic recipe. Serve with Oven-Roasted Tomato Sauce (page 70).

2 tablespoons olive oil
1 medium-size yellow onion, sliced as thinly as possible
Kosher salt
One 10-ounce package fresh spinach, stemmed, leaves rinsed in
    several changes of cold water, or one 10-ounce
    package frozen chopped spinach, defrosted
½ cup whole-milk ricotta cheese
⅓ cup freshly grated Parmesan cheese, plus extra for serving
1 large egg, lightly beaten
Freshly ground black pepper

Heat the oil in a medium-size skillet over medium heat. Add the onion; season with salt to taste. Reduce the heat to medium-low; cook, stirring occasionally, until the onion is golden brown, 25 to 30 minutes.

Place the washed spinach in a large pot. Cover and steam until the leaves are tender, 5 minutes. (If you are using frozen spinach, cook according to the directions on the package.) Transfer the cooked spinach to a wire mesh strainer and using a fork, press the excess water from the spinach. Chop the spinach. In a small mixing bowl, combine the spinach with the ricotta, Parmesan, egg, salt, and pepper to taste. Add the caramelized onion; stir well to combine all the ingredients.

Fill and cook ravioli according to instructions on pages 218–19.

POTATO AND FUNGHI PORCINI RAVIOLI

ABOUT 1½ CUPS

This is a wonderful recipe from Turin in northwestern Italy. Serve these ravioli lightly coated with Butter and Crispy Sage Sauce (recipe follows).

1 ounce dry porcini mushrooms or other dry mushrooms
¼ cup olive oil
⅓ cup finely chopped onion
1 clove garlic, pressed or finely minced
¾ pound boiling potatoes, peeled and cut into 2-inch pieces
Kosher salt

Place the dry mushrooms in a heat-proof glass measuring cup. Cover with boiling water; allow to stand 30 minutes. Drain, reserving the liquid, and finely chop the mushrooms. Strain the liquid through a double thickness of paper towels; set aside.

In a small skillet, heat the oil over medium heat. Add the onion and garlic. Cook, stirring frequently, until the onion is lightly browned, about 15 minutes.

Meanwhile, place the potatoes in a small saucepan with water to cover; bring to a boil over medium-high heat. Reduce the heat to medium. Cook until the potatoes are tender when pierced with a fork, about 15 minutes; drain. Mash the potatoes through a ricer or strainer or with a potato masher. Do not put potatoes in a food processor, as it will turn them to a paste.

In a small mixing bowl, combine the mashed potatoes with the onions, mushrooms, salt to taste, and 2 tablespoons of the mushroom soaking liquid; stir well to combine.

Fill and cook ravioli according to instructions on pages 218–19.

❖ BUTTER AND CRISPY SAGE SAUCE

ABOUT ⅓ CUP

Sage is a traditional ingredient in Northern Italian dishes. In ancient times, sage was associated with good health—the Italian word for sage, *salvia*, comes from the Latin *salvere*, which means "to be of good health."

¼ cup (½ stick) unsalted butter
2 tablespoons olive oil
12 fresh sage leaves
Freshly grated Parmesan cheese

While the ravioli are cooking, heat the butter and oil in a large skillet over medium-high heat. When the butter begins to bubble, add the sage leaves. Cook until the leaves are crisp, about 10 minutes. When the ravioli are cooked, drain and add to the skillet with the butter and sage leaves. Toss well; serve with Parmesan.

◈ SWISS CHARD, RICOTTA, AND MASCARPONE RAVIOLI

1½ CUPS

Swiss chard, a relative of the beet root, is a staple of Italian cooking and filled pasta dishes. You can use both the leaves and stems of chard in cooking, although this recipe calls only for the leaves. Save the stalks and add them to soups or stir-fries. If chard is not available, substitute fresh spinach, chopped frozen spinach, or beet greens. Serve with Sicilian Pesto (recipe follows) or with a simple sauce of butter and Parmesan.

1 large bunch Swiss chard, leaves only, stems removed and
    reserved for another use, tough ribs pulled from the leaves
    (about 10 ounces cleaned leaves), and rinsed in cold water
⅓ cup whole-milk ricotta cheese
¼ cup mascarpone cheese
Kosher salt
¼ cup freshly grated Parmesan cheese

Place the wet chard leaves in a large saucepan. Cover and place over medium-high heat. Cook until the chard is tender, 5 to 7 minutes. Transfer the chard to a wire mesh strainer and, using a fork, press out any excess water in the leaves. Place the leaves in a food processor; process until finely chopped, about 15 seconds, or chop by hand. Add the ricotta, mascarpone, and salt to taste. Turn the processor on and off to combine. Transfer to a small mixing bowl; stir in the Parmesan.

Fill and cook the ravioli according to the instructions on pages 218–19.

▦ SICILIAN PESTO SAUCE

ABOUT ¾ CUP

Almonds make the difference in this Sicilian-style basil pesto.

2 cups fresh basil leaves
¼ cup blanched almonds
1 clove garlic, peeled
½ teaspoon kosher salt
½ cup extra virgin olive oil

In a food processor fitted with a metal blade or in a blender, combine the basil, almonds, garlic, and salt; process until the mixture is finely chopped, about 20 seconds. Scrape the sides down and process about 5 seconds longer. With the machine running, gradually add the olive oil. Continue processing about 10 seconds longer until sauce is smooth.

ARTICHOKE RAVIOLI WITH LEMON CREAM SAUCE

ABOUT 2 CUPS

This recipe, from my friend Holly Safford, are perfectly complemented by the Lemon Cream Sauce (recipe follows).

8 ounces frozen artichoke hearts, defrosted and finely chopped
1 cup whole-milk ricotta cheese
4 ounces mozzarella cheese, shredded
$\frac{1}{2}$ cup freshly grated Parmesan cheese
$\frac{1}{4}$ cup grated aged Asiago cheese
3 tablespoons chopped fresh basil leaves
2 large cloves garlic, pressed or finely minced
2 tablespoons chopped fresh parsley
2 large egg yolks, lightly beaten
2 large eggs, lightly beaten

Combine all the ingredients in a large mixing bowl. Mix until well incorporated and pale green in color.

Fill and cook the ravioli according to the instructions on pages 218–19.

Lemon Cream Sauce

ABOUT 3 CUPS

4 cups heavy cream
$\frac{1}{4}$ cup grated lemon zest
$\frac{1}{2}$ cup freshly grated Parmesan cheese
Kosher salt
Freshly ground black pepper
$\frac{1}{4}$ cup chopped fresh chives

Pour the cream into a small saucepan and place over medium heat; bring to a simmer. Cook, stirring occasionally, until the cream is reduced to about half, about 10 minutes. Add the lemon zest and Parmesan; simmer 10 minutes. Add salt and pepper to taste. Stir in ¼ cup of the chives. Sauce the ravioli on individual serving plates and garnish with the remaining chives.

CARAMELIZED LEEK AND ONION WITH GOAT CHEESE RAVIOLI

1½ CUPS

The sweetness of the onion and leek is offset by the sharp flavor of the goat cheese. Use any fresh (not aged) unflavored goat cheese; the creamy American-made varieties work particularly well. Serve with a sauce of garlicky spinach and roasted figs (see page 80).

¼ cup olive oil
1 large Bermuda onion (about ¾ pound), cut in half and thinly
   sliced (2½ to 3 cups sliced)
2 medium-size leeks (white part only), rinsed well between the
   layers to remove any sand or grit and cut into matchstick strips
Kosher salt
4 ounces fresh goat cheese

Heat the oil in a large skillet over medium heat. Add the onion and leeks; season with salt to taste. Reduce the heat to medium-low; cook, stirring occasionally, until the leeks and onion are golden brown, 30 to 40 minutes.

Crumble the goat cheese in a small mixing bowl. Add the

caramelized onion and leeks and, using a fork, mash the mixture to combine.

Fill and cook the ravioli according to the instructions on pages 218–19.

▣ BASIL AND GOAT CHEESE RAVIOLI

ABOUT 1½ CUPS

The goat cheese and pesto make a marvelously flavorful filling. Prepare the Ligurian eggless pasta dough for the wrappers (see page 12) and serve with garlic, oil, hot red pepper, and parsley (page 48).

6 ounces fresh, unflavored goat cheese
5 tablespoons Fresh Pesto Sauce (see page 112)
¼ cup freshly grated Parmesan cheese

In a small mixing bowl combine the goat cheese, pesto, and Parmesan. Using a fork, stir the mixture until it has a smooth, creamy consistency.

Fill and cook the ravioli according to the directions on pages 218–19.

PUMPKIN NUTMEG AND RICOTTA RAVIOLI

ABOUT 1½ CUPS

A classic Lombardian dish, ravioli with pumpkin filling can be suprisingly sweet tasting. This version is more savory than sweet and very rich. Serve with Garlic-and-Sage-Flavored Butter Sauce (recipe follows).

2 pounds fresh pumpkin or Hubbard squash, peeled, seeded, and cut into 2-inch pieces or use unsweetened, canned pumpkin, drained
⅓ cup whole-milk ricotta cheese
¼ cup freshly grated Parmesan cheese
Pinch of ground nutmeg
Kosher salt
Freshly ground black pepper

Place the pumpkin in a medium-size saucepan with water to cover; bring to a boil over medium-high heat. Reduce the heat to medium-low; simmer until the pumpkin is tender when pierced with a sharp knife, about 20 minutes. Drain and place the cooked (or canned) pumpkin in a food processor fitted with the double-edge steel blade. Process until smooth, about 30 seconds. Add the ricotta, Parmesan, nutmeg, and salt and pepper to taste. Process to combine the ingredients, another 10 seconds.

Fill and cook the ravioli according to the directions on pages 218–19.

Garlic-and-Sage-Flavored Butter Sauce

6 SERVINGS

6 tablespoons (³/₄ stick) unsalted butter
1 clove garlic, pressed or finely minced
6 fresh sage leaves
Freshly grated Parmesan cheese

Melt the butter in a large skillet over medium heat until it begins to bubble. Add the garlic and sage; cook 1 minute. Turn off the heat and add the ravioli. Shake the pan back and forth to coat the ravioli evenly with the butter. Transfer the ravioli to individual serving bowls. Top each serving with one of the sage leaves. Serve in preheated individual serving bowls with Parmesan.

RADICCHIO RAVIOLI WITH RADICCHIO AND BUTTER SAUCE

ABOUT 1¹/₂ CUPS

The bitter taste of radicchio, or red chicory, becomes quite mild when cooked. These ravioli are particularly nice when served with shredded radicchio that has been sautéed in butter.

¹/₄ cup olive oil
¹/₂ cup finely chopped onion (1 small onion)
1 small head radicchio (about ¹/₂ pound), shredded (about 2 cups)
Kosher salt
¹/₂ cup whole-milk ricotta cheese
2 tablespoons mascarpone cheese
1 large egg, lightly beaten
1 tablespoon freshly grated Parmesan cheese

Heat the oil in a medium-size skillet over medium-high heat. Add the onion. Cook until the onion begins to soften, 2 to 3 minutes. Add the radicchio; season with salt to taste. Reduce the heat to medium; cook until the radicchio is completely tender and any liquid in the pan has evaporated, about 10 minutes. The radicchio will turn a rosy purple color.

Transfer the radicchio to a small mixing bowl. Add the ricotta, mascarpone, egg, and Parmesan; mix well with a wooden spoon. Fill and cook the ravioli according to the instructions on pages 218–19.

BUTTER AND RADICCHIO SAUCE

6 SERVINGS

6 tablespoons (³⁄₄ cup) unsalted butter
1 cup shredded radicchio
Kosher salt
Freshly grated Parmesan cheese

Heat the butter in a large skillet over medium heat. When it becomes bubbly, add the radicchio; season with salt to taste. Cook, stirring, until the radicchio is barely tender, about 5 minutes. Turn off the heat and set aside. When the ravioli are cooked and drained, add them to the skillet with the butter and radicchio; toss well. Serve with Parmesan.

ZUCCHINI, SUMMER SQUASH, AND THREE CHEESE RAVIOLI

1½ CUPS

This filling has a delicate, but definite flavor of zucchini, and the creamy cheeses make it deliciously rich. If summer squash is not available, substitute more zucchini in its place. Serve with Fresh Tomato Sauce (page 86) or lightly coated with melted unsalted butter and lots of fresh Parmesan cheese.

¼ cup olive oil
1 clove garlic, pressed or finely minced
2 cups diced zucchini (about ¾ pound)
1 cup diced summer squash (about ½ pound)
Kosher salt
4 ounces fresh whole-milk mozzarella, cut into small dice
¼ cup whole-milk ricotta cheese
3 tablespoons freshly grated Parmesan cheese

Heat the oil in a medium-size skillet over medium-high heat. Add the garlic, zucchini, and summer squash; season with salt. Cook, stirring occasionally, until the squash is completely tender, about 7 minutes. Transfer to a food processor fitted with a doubled-edged steel blade. Process until the squash is finely chopped, but not pureed, about 15 seconds. Add the cheeses. Turn the processor on and off until the ingredients are combined well.

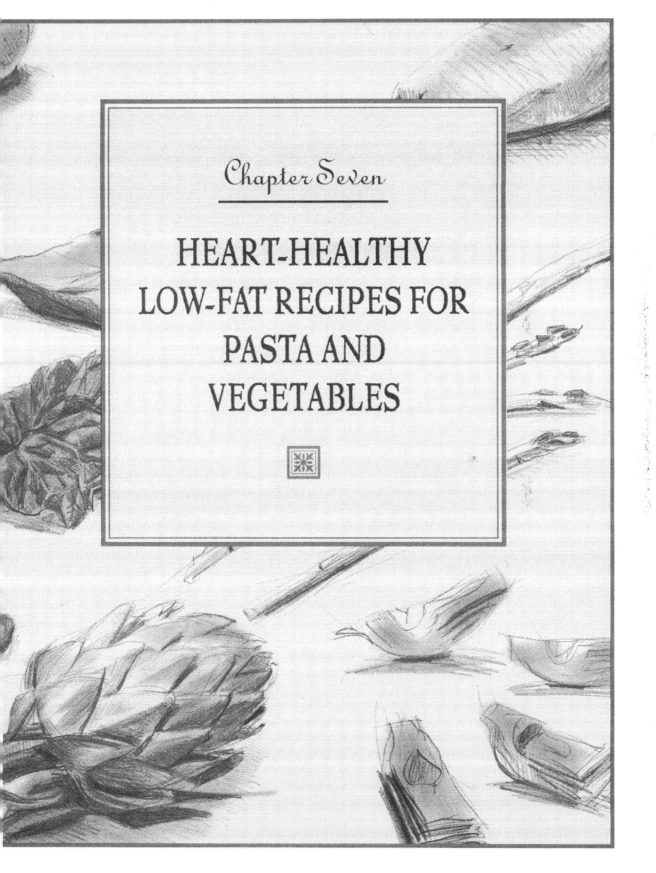

Chapter Seven

HEART-HEALTHY LOW-FAT RECIPES FOR PASTA AND VEGETABLES

This chapter was inspired by some friends who are, for health reasons, always in search of very low- and no-fat recipes. At the outset, I knew that some obvious sources of fat could be reduced or even eliminated. Just cutting my typical ¼ cup olive oil in a recipe to 1 or 2 tablespoons significantly reduces fat. Skim or low-fat milk can be substituted for whole milk in the recipes calling for béchamel sauce. Skim-milk mozzarella and ricotta can be used in place of whole-milk cheese. Wine or broth are a substitute for oil for sautéing some ingredients; and potato, bean, and other vegetable purees can be used to thicken and enrich sauces and soups—two techniques I learned on my visits to a health spa where the food tasted genuinely delicious.

What I quickly discovered is that the taste of recipes with little or no fat is significantly different from that of dishes rich with oil. They are lighter both in texture and taste, and that takes some getting used to. But happily, they are also very flavorful. Dishes that don't have a pronounced taste of the oil have more of the taste of the ingredients, in this case, the pasta and vegetables. I found that there's more mushroomy flavor in a low-fat mushroom sauce; more taste of tomatoes in the spa-style tomato sauce.

I have tried to make these low-fat recipes appealing to everyone;

ABOUT OILS

Although olive oil is unquestionably the primary oil used in Italian cooking, other vegetable and seed oils, called *olio di semi*, made from a blend of rapeseed and sunflower seed oils, are also used and are particularly popular in Italy. Other oils used, to a lesser degree, by Italian cooks include corn and peanut oils. Canola oil is rated the lowest in cholesterol, and you can substitute it for olive oil in the recipes without changing the texture or the consistency of the dish. You will, though, lose the olive oil flavor.

even those who are not strictly observant of low-fat diets can enjoy them too. The sprinkling of Parmesan cheese adds much flavor to these sauces, but it also adds some fat, 2 grams per tablespoon, so I have listed it as optional in each recipe. I call for dry eggless pasta in all the recipes. Fresh pasta is almost always prepared with eggs, which are high in cholesterol, whereas dry pasta is usually made only with flour and water. If you want to use fresh pasta, prepare the Ligurian Eggless Pasta (page 12).

LOW-FAT FETTUCINE PRIMAVERA

6 SERVINGS

Primavera means spring in Italian and to me the vegetables most closely associated with springtime are asparagus, fresh leeks, baby peas, and sweet carrots. You can substitute other vegetables to suit your own taste, just keep the quantities approximately the same so you don't end up with a sauce that overwhelms the pasta.

1 pound dry fettucine or linguine

2 tablespoons olive oil

2 tablespoons chopped red onion

1 clove garlic, pressed or finely minced

1 small leek, white part only, rinsed well between the layers to
remove any grit or sand and cut into julienne strips ($1/2$ cup)

1 small carrot, cut into julienne strips (about $1/2$ cup)

$1/2$ pound asparagus, tough bottoms cut off, cut into 2-inch
lengths, keeping the tips whole

$1/2$ cup fresh shelled baby peas or frozen peas, defrosted

$1/3$ cup broth (see pages 121–26)

2 tablespoons chopped fresh parsley

12 fresh chives, cut into 2-inch lengths

Salt, optional

Freshly grated Parmesan cheese for serving (optional)

Bring a large pot of water to a rolling boil over high heat. Add the fettucine. Cook, stirring occasionally, until the pasta is tender but firm, *al dente*, 7 to 10 minutes. Drain.

While the pasta is cooking, heat the oil in a large skillet over medium heat. Add the onion, garlic, leek, and carrot; season with salt to taste. Cook until the leek and carrot are tender, about 5 to 7 minutes. Add the asparagus, fresh peas, if you are using them, and broth. Cook exactly 5 minutes. (If you are using frozen peas, add them after the asparagus and cook 1 minute more.)

Transfer the pasta to a large preheated serving bowl. Pour the vegetables over the pasta; toss well. Garnish with the chives and parsley; season with salt and serve with Parmesan, if desired.

Tip: When cooking low-fat recipes, you'll get the best results if you use a saucepan or skillet with a nonstick surface.

PENNE WITH ZUCCHINI, SUMMER SQUASH, AND SPA-STYLE NO-FAT MARINARA SAUCE

6 SERVINGS

This recipe makes a colorful, hearty dish. If summer squash is not available, substitute additional zucchini.

$\frac{1}{2}$ cup dry white wine
1 small onion, finely chopped
1 medium-size carrot, finely chopped
2 tablespoons chopped celery
2 cloves garlic, pressed or finely minced
3 cups chopped canned tomatoes with their juice
1 tablespoon kosher salt, plus extra for seasoning
2 tablespoons chopped fresh oregano leaves
1 tablespoon chopped fresh basil leaves
1 tablespoon chopped fresh parsley leaves
1 pound dry penne
1 medium-size green zucchini (about $\frac{1}{2}$ pound), ends cut off
    and discarded, and cut into julienne strips
1 medium-size summer squash (about $\frac{1}{2}$ pound), ends cut off
    and discarded, and cut into julienne strips
Freshly grated Parmesan cheese (optional)

Combine the wine, onion, carrot, celery, and garlic in a large saucepan. Cook over medium heat until the wine is almost evaporated and the onion is translucent, about 10 minutes. Add the chopped tomatoes. Reduce the heat to medium-low; continue cooking, stirring occasionally, until the carrots are tender, 20 to 25 minutes longer. Transfer the sauce to a food processor fitted with a metal blade or blender; process until the mixture is smooth, about 30 seconds. Return the tomato sauce to the saucepan; add salt to taste. Reheat before serving. In a small mixing bowl, combine the herbs and set aside.

Bring a large pot of water to a rolling boil over high heat. Add the penne. Cook, stirring occasionally, 3 minutes. Add the zucchini and summer squash. Cook until the pasta is tender but firm, *al dente*, about 5 minutes longer. Drain and transfer to individual preheated pasta plates. Top each serving with about ¹/₂ cup of the sauce and a sprinkling of the herbs for garnish. Serve with Parmesan, if desired.

PENNE WITH ARTICHOKES, POTATOES, AND SPINACH

4 SERVINGS

The lemon and garlic give the artichokes and spinach in this sauce a surprising boost of flavor, while the potatoes provide heartiness and substance. Serve it with a dusting of Parmesan for some added flavor.

2 medium-size artichokes

1 tablespoon olive oil

1 large clove garlic, pressed or finely minced

1 medium-size boiling potato, preferably Yukon Gold, peeled
   and cut into 2-inch julienne strips

Juice of $\frac{1}{2}$ lemon

1 cup cold water

3 cups coarsely chopped fresh spinach leaves, rinsed well in
   several changes of cold water, and dried

$\frac{1}{2}$ pound dry penne

Salt, optional

Freshly grated Parmesan cheese (optional)

For each artichoke, peel away the tough dark green leaves until
only the yellow-green leaves are visible. Do not use scissors or a
knife for this; the leaves will break naturally at the point where the
tough part ends and the tender part begins. Use a serrated knife to
cut 1 to 2 inches off the top of the artichoke. Use a small paring
knife to peel the stem and trim around the base. Cut the artichokes
into quarters lengthwise and cut out the chokes. Slice the artichoke quarters lengthwise as thinly as possible.

Heat the oil in a small skillet over medium-high heat. Add the
artichokes, garlic, and potatoes. Cook, stirring, about 2 minutes.
Add the lemon juice and water. Bring to a boil; reduce the heat to
medium-low. Cover the pan and simmer until the artichokes are
tender and most of the water has evaporated, about 20 minutes.
Turn off the heat and set aside. (The artichokes and potatoes can
be prepared to this point up to several hours in advance.)

Bring a large pot of water to a rolling boil over high heat. Add
the penne. Cook, stirring occasionally, until the penne is tender
but firm, *al dente*, 7 to 10 minutes. While the pasta is cooking,

reheat the artichokes and potatoes, adding a little warm water if they seem too dry, over medium-low heat. Add the chopped spinach. Cook until the spinach is tender, about 5 minutes. Drain the pasta; transfer to a preheated serving dish. Pour the artichoke and spinach mixture over the pasta; toss well. Season with salt and serve with Parmesan, if desired.

Tip: When using oil for sautéing ingredients in low-fat recipes, try wiping the surface of the skillet or saucepan with a paper towel that's been dipped in olive oil. Or try using olive oil spray from a can, which can be purchased in the supermarket. You'll use a lot less oil.

◼ PENNE WITH FRESH TOMATOES, LEEKS, AND ROASTED ARTICHOKE HEARTS

SERVES 4 TO 6

This recipe was inspired by a dish I ate at the Canyon Ranch health spa, in Lennox, Massachusetts. Use frozen artichoke hearts and defrost before roasting them in the oven.

3 pounds fresh, ripe plum tomatoes
1 tablespoon olive oil
2 cloves garlic, peeled and pressed or finely minced
1 large leek, white part only, root end discarded, cut in half
    lengthwise, rinsed well, and thinly sliced crosswise
    (to yield 2 cups)
¼ cup dry white wine or water
¼ cup tomato puree or chopped canned tomatoes
2 tablespoons chopped fresh parsley leaves
One 9-ounce package frozen artichoke hearts, defrosted and cut
    in half, lengthwise
Olive oil spray or 1 tablespoon olive oil
1 pound dry penne
Salt, optional
Freshly grated Parmesan cheese (optional)

Bring 2 quarts of water to a boil in a large saucepan over high heat. Place the tomatoes in the boiling water. Wait 1 minute; drain. Place them in a colander to cool slightly. Use a sharp paring knife to cut away the stem end of the tomato and peel off the skin. The skin should slip off easily; if it does not, place the tomato back into the boiling water for 30 seconds longer. Holding the peeled tomato in one hand, cut around the inside core; gently squeeze out the core and seeds. Hold the tomato under cold water to flush out any remaining seeds. Set aside. Coarsely chop the tomatoes.

Combine the olive oil and garlic in a large saucepan over medium-high heat. Cook about 1 minute, until the garlic begins to sizzle. Add the leeks and the wine. Cook, stirring frequently until the leeks begin to soften and the wine has mostly evaporated. Add the tomatoes; season with salt to taste. Stir well with a wooden spoon. Continue cooking 10 to 15 minutes longer, stirring frequently, until the leek and tomatoes have cooked into a thick sauce. Add the tomato puree. Cook about 5 minutes longer. Stir in the parsley. Turn off the heat and set aside.

Preheat the oven to 500°F. Arrange the artichoke hearts in a single layer in a medium-size roasting pan lined with aluminum foil. Lightly spray or brush the artichokes with olive oil. Sprinkle with kosher salt, if desired. Roast in the oven for 10 minutes. Remove from the oven; set aside.

Bring a large pot of water to a rolling boil over high heat. Add the penne. Cook, stirring occasionally, 7 to 10 minutes until the pasta is tender but firm, *al dente*. Drain; transfer to a large preheated serving bowl. Add the leek and tomato sauce and the artichokes. Toss well to combine. Serve with Parmesan.

▦ SPAGHETTINI WITH LOW-FAT TOMATO AND BASIL SAUCE

SERVES 4 TO 6

This light variation on traditional fresh tomato sauce has a lot of great tomato flavor and a very rich taste.

3 pounds fresh, ripe plum tomatoes
1 tablespoon olive oil
2 cloves garlic, peeled and pressed or finely minced
Kosher salt, optional
1 cup chopped canned plum tomatoes
$\frac{1}{3}$ cup finely chopped fresh basil leaves
$\frac{1}{4}$ cup finely chopped fresh parsley
1 pound dry spaghettini
Freshly grated Parmesan cheese (optional)

Bring 2 quarts of water to a boil in a large saucepan over high heat. Place the tomatoes in the boiling water. Wait 1 minute; drain and place them in a colander to cool slightly. Use a sharp paring knife to cut away the stem end of the tomato and peel off the skin. The skin should slip off easily; if it does not, place the tomato back into the boiling water for 30 seconds longer. Holding the peeled tomato in one hand, cut around the inside core; gently squeeze out the core and seeds. Hold the tomato under cold water to flush out any remaining seeds. Set aside. Coarsely chop the tomatoes.

Combine the oil and garlic in a large saucepan over medium-high heat. Cook about 1 minute until the garlic begins to sizzle. Add the chopped tomatoes; season with salt, if desired. Stir well with a wooden spoon. Continue cooking 7 to 10 minutes or longer, stirring frequently, until the tomatoes have cooked into a sauce. Add the canned tomatoes. Turn the heat to medium; cook about 10 minutes longer. Stir in the basil and parsley. Turn off the heat and set aside. Reheat before serving.

Bring a large pot of water to a rolling boil over high heat. Add a tablespoon of salt and the spaghettini. Cook, stirring occasionally, 7 to 10 minutes until the pasta is tender but firm, *al dente*. Drain; transfer to individual preheated serving bowls. Top each serving with about $1/2$ cup of the tomato sauce. Serve with Parmesan.

SPAGHETTINI WITH ROASTED SWEET RED PEPPER SAUCE

4 SERVINGS

This is a sauce for pepper lovers. The natural sweetness and flavor of the red pepper is very intense. I like to serve it with grated Asiago cheese, which has a more pungent flavor than Parmesan and delicately offsets the sweetness of the pepper. You also can use grated Parmesan cheese.

1 medium-size red bell pepper
1 tablespoon olive oil
1 large clove garlic, pressed or finely minced
1 small onion, finely chopped (to yield about $1/4$ cup)
1 cup canned crushed or ground peeled tomatoes
Kosher salt, optional
Pinch of red pepper flakes
$1/2$ pound dry spaghettini
$1/4$ cup chopped fresh parsley leaves
$1/3$ cup grated fresh Asiago cheese (optional)

Preheat the oven broiler. Cut the pepper in half lengthwise. Remove the seeds and core; place, cut side down, on an aluminum foil-lined baking sheet. Place under the broiler on the topmost rack; broil until the pepper is completely black, about 8 minutes. Remove from the oven; cover loosely with foil. Allow to stand 10 minutes. Use your fingers and peel the pepper under cold running water. The skin should come off easily. Pat dry with a paper towel and chop.

Heat the oil in a medium-size skillet over medium heat. Add the garlic and onion. Cook, stirring, until the onion begins to soften, 2 to 3 minutes. Add the pepper and continue cooking about 5 minutes longer. Add the tomatoes, salt to taste, and the red pepper flakes. Reduce the heat to medium-low; simmer 20 minutes longer, stirring occasionally. Transfer the pepper and tomato sauce to a food processor fitted with a metal blade or to a blender; process until smooth, about 30 seconds. Return to the skillet and reheat before serving.

Bring a large pot of water to a rolling boil over high heat. Add the spaghettini. Cook, stirring occasionally, until the pasta is tender but firm, *al dente*, 5 to 7 minutes. Drain; transfer to individual preheated serving plates. Top each serving with some of the pepper-and-tomato sauce, a sprinkling of parsley, and some Asiago cheese.

▦ ZITI WITH EGGPLANT, ZUCCHINI, AND TOMATO SAUCE

4 TO 6 SERVINGS

This sauce is very reminiscent of a *ratatouille*, but the addition of lots of fresh basil gives it a distinctly Italian taste. For the best flavor, simmer this sauce for a good long while. You can't overcook it.

1 medium-size eggplant (1 to 1$\frac{1}{2}$ pounds), stem end cut off and discarded, cut into 1-inch cubes
$\frac{1}{2}$ pound zucchini, stem end cut off and discarded, cut into quarters, lengthwise, and sliced crosswise into $\frac{1}{2}$-inch thick slices
Kosher salt, optional
1 tablespoon olive oil
1 large onion, peeled and diced
1 large clove garlic, pressed or finely minced
1 cup chopped canned tomatoes
Freshly ground black pepper
$\frac{1}{4}$ cup finely chopped fresh basil leaves
1 pound dry ziti
Freshly grated Parmesan cheese (optional)

Place the eggplant and zucchini in a large colander. Sprinkle lightly with salt and allow to stand and drain about 30 minutes.

Combine the olive oil with the onion and garlic in a heavy, 4-quart casserole with a tight-fitting lid. Place over medium high heat; cook 2 to 3 minutes until the onion begins to soften. Add the eggplant and zucchini. Continue cooking, while stirring, 2 to 3 minutes longer. Add the chopped tomatoes; stir well to combine. Turn the heat to medium-low. Cover the casserole and simmer about 45 minutes, stirring occasionally, until the eggplant is completely tender. Stir in the basil. Turn off the heat and set aside. Reheat before serving.

Bring a large pot of water to a rolling boil over high heat. Add the ziti. Cook, stirring occasionally, 7 to 10 minutes until the pasta is tender but firm, *al dente*. Drain and transfer to a large preheated serving bowl. Add the sauce; toss well. Serve with freshly grated Parmesan.

FUSILLI WITH ZUCCHINI AND GARLIC SAUCE

6 SERVINGS

A great way to cook up some of those late-summer overgrown zucchini. The grated zucchini makes a thick and rich-tasting sauce, even with little added fat in the recipe. For an even thicker sauce you can puree the cooked zucchini.

2 pounds zucchini, ends cut off and discarded
1 tablespoon olive oil
2 large cloves garlic, pressed or finely minced
Kosher salt, optional
1 pound dry fusilli
1/4 cup chopped fresh basil leaves
2 tablespoons chopped fresh parsley leaves
Freshly grated Parmesan cheese (optional)

Use your food processor or a standing four-sided grater and coarsely grate the zucchini. Heat the oil in a large skillet over medium-high heat. Add the garlic and grated zucchini. Cook, stirring, until the zucchini is tender and most of the liquid in the pan has evaporated, 7 to 10 minutes. Season with salt, if desired.

Bring a large pot of water to a rolling boil over high heat. Add the tablespoon of salt and the fusilli. Cook, stirring occasionally, until the pasta is tender but firm, *al dente*, 7 to 10 minutes. Drain; transfer to a large preheated serving bowl. Pour the zucchini over the pasta. Add the basil and parsley; toss well. Serve with Parmesan.

FETTUCINE WITH MUSHROOMS AND BABY WHITE ONIONS

6 SERVINGS

A hearty and richly flavored sauce that is so good no one will believe it is low in fat. Use baby white or pearl onions to add delicate onion flavor, and a well-seasoned broth to give this sauce even more good taste.

1 ounce dried porcini mushrooms (or other dried mushrooms
   such as shiitake or cepes)
$\frac{1}{2}$ cup broth (see pages 121–26)
2 large cloves garlic, pressed or finely minced
1 pound mushrooms (preferably portobello, crimini, or shiitake),
   stemmed and caps thinly sliced (about 4 cups sliced)
6 small white onions, peeled and cut into quarters
1 tablespoon kosher salt, plus extra for seasoning
Freshly ground black pepper
1 pound dry fettucine, linguine, or other long pasta
1 tablespoon extra virgin olive oil
2 tablespoons chopped fresh parsley leaves

Place the dried mushrooms in a heat-proof glass measuring cup. Fill it with boiling water and allow to stand 20 minutes. Drain, reserving ½ cup of the liquid. Coarsely chop the mushrooms. Strain the reserved mushroom liquid through a double thickness of paper towels.

Combine the mushroom liquid with the broth and garlic in a medium-size saucepan over medium-high heat. Add the chopped dried mushrooms, the sliced fresh mushrooms, and onions; season with salt and pepper to taste, if desired. Reduce the heat to medium-low; cover and cook 10 minutes. Uncover the pan and cook until the sauce is thick and most of the liquid has evaporated, about 5 minutes longer. Turn off the heat. Cover to keep warm and set aside.

Bring a large pot of water to a rolling boil over high heat. Add the fettucine. Cook, stirring occasionally, until the pasta is tender but firm, *al dente*, 7 to 10 minutes. Drain; transfer to a large pre-heated serving bowl. Pour the mushroom sauce over the pasta. Drizzle the olive oil over the sauce and garnish with the chopped parsley. Toss well and serve immediately.

PENNE WITH LENTILS, TOMATOES, AND MUSHROOMS

4 SERVINGS

This is a hearty and satisfying dish that makes the perfect center-piece to a rustic winter dinner. If you intend to prepare it ahead of time, you'll need to add some additional broth to the sauce before reheating it.

½ cup dried lentils, picked over and rinsed

2 cups cold water

1 tablespoon olive oil

2 tablespoons chopped onion

1 large clove garlic, pressed or finely minced

½ pound mushrooms (preferably portobello, crimini, or shiitake), stemmed, and caps thinly sliced (to yield about 2 cups)

Kosher salt, optional

¼ teaspoon red pepper flakes

½ cup broth (see page 121–26)

½ cup chopped canned tomatoes with their juice

½ pound dry penne

2 tablespoons chopped fresh parsley leaves

Freshly grated Parmesan cheese (optional)

Combine the lentils and water in a small saucepan. Cover and place over high heat. When the water comes to a boil, reduce the heat to medium-low; simmer until the lentils are completely tender, about 35 minutes. Drain in a colander; set aside.

Heat the oil in a medium-size skillet over medium-high heat. Add the onion and garlic. Cook, stirring constantly, until the onion begins to soften, 2 to 3 minutes. Add the mushrooms; season with salt, if desired, and the red pepper flakes. Stir to combine with the oil and onion. Add the broth. Reduce the heat to medium-low; simmer until the mushrooms are tender and about half the broth has evaporated, about 7 to 10 minutes. Add the lentils and tomatoes. Cook about 10 minutes longer.

Meanwhile, bring a large pot of water to a rolling boil over high heat. Add the penne. Cook, stirring occasionally, until the pasta is tender but firm, al dente, 7 to 10 minutes. Drain; transfer to a large preheated serving bowl. Pour the sauce over the pasta. Add the parsley; toss well before serving. Serve with Parmesan.

BOW TIES WITH ESCAROLE, WHITE BEANS, AND GARLIC

4 SERVINGS

This sauce has a lot of great flavor, but it's best served as soon as it is cooked.

½ pound bow ties
2 tablespoons olive oil
2 cloves garlic, pressed or finely minced
4 cups shredded escarole leaves
1 cup dried white kidney beans, cooked according to directions
    on pages 127–29, or one 16-ounce can cannellini beans, drained
    and rinsed well
¼ cup broth (see pages 121–26)
Kosher salt, optional
Freshly grated Parmesan cheese (optional)

Bring a large pot of water to a rolling boil over high heat. Add the bow ties. Cook, stirring occasionally, until the pasta is tender but firm, *al dente*, 7 to 10 minutes. Drain.

While the pasta is cooking, heat the olive oil in a medium-size skillet over medium-high heat. Add the garlic and escarole. Cook until the escarole is wilted, 1 to 2 minutes. Add the beans and broth. Cook until the beans are heated through. Season with salt, if desired.

Transfer the pasta to a large preheated serving bowl. Add the escarole and white beans; toss well. Serve with Parmesan.

❖ BOW TIES WITH CREAMY FENNEL, BROCCOLI, AND SPINACH SAUCE

4 SERVINGS

This light vegetable puree makes a delicious sauce for pasta. It's also a great way to use up broccoli stalks that you never know what to do with. For a more substantial dish, add some cooked broccoli florets to the finished dish.

1 small fresh fennel bulb (about ½ pound), stalks and leaves removed and discarded, bulb cut into 1-inch pieces
1 pound broccoli stalks, peeled and cut into 1-inch pieces
2 cups packed fresh spinach leaves, stemmed, and rinsed well in cold water but not dried
1 tablespoon olive oil
Kosher salt
Freshly ground black pepper
½ pound dry bow ties

Combine the fennel and broccoli in a small saucepan with just enough water to cover. Bring to a boil over medium-high heat; turn heat to low and simmer about 10 minutes until the fennel is tender. Add the spinach; stir to combine. Cook 1 minute until the spinach is wilted and tender. Drain the vegetables, reserving the cooking liquid.

Place the vegetables in the container of a food processor or blender; process about 30 seconds until smooth. Add the liquid, ¼ cup at a time until the puree is the consistency of a thick soup. Add the olive oil; process about 10 seconds. Season with salt and pepper to taste, if desired. Transfer the puree to the saucepan. Reheat before serving.

Bring a large pot of water to a rolling boil over high heat. Add the bow ties. Cook, stirring occasionally, 7 to 10 minutes until the pasta is tender but firm, *al dente*. Drain; transfer to a large, preheated serving bowl. Add the fennel and broccoli sauce; toss well before serving.

▦ LINGUINE WITH LOW-FAT PESTO SAUCE

4 TO 6 SERVINGS

Basil and garlic give this sauce its pesto flavor, and the steamed spinach inconspicuously makes it thick. Serve with some Parmesan cheese, if your diet allows.

2 cups packed fresh spinach leaves, stemmed, rinsed well in
   several changes of cold water, but not dried
1 cup packed fresh basil leaves, stemmed
1 clove garlic, peeled
Kosher salt, optional
1 tablespoon olive oil (optional)
1 pound dry linguine
Freshly grated Parmesan cheese (optional)

Place the rinsed spinach leaves in a small saucepan. Cover the pot and place over medium-high heat. Cook until the spinach is tender, about 5 minutes. Transfer the spinach and its cooking liquid to a food processor fitted with a metal blade. Add the basil leaves, garlic, and salt to taste, if desired. Process until the sauce is smooth, about 15 seconds. Scrape the sides down and process a few seconds longer. With the machine running, gradually add the olive oil to the spinach and basil mixture. The mixture should be thick and smooth. If the sauce is too thick, add some water a tablespoon at a time, with the machine running, until it reaches the desired consistency.

Bring a large pot of water to a rolling boil over high heat. Add the linguine. Cook, stirring occasionally, until the pasta is tender but firm, *al dente*, 7 to 10 minutes. Drain; transfer to a large preheated serving bowl. Add the pesto; toss well. Season with salt to taste. Serve with Parmesan, if desired.

LEAN LASAGNA

6 TO 8 SERVINGS

When I visited the Albergo del Sole, an inn and restaurant in Maleo in Lombardy, I was served a delicious vegetable lasagna with a multitude of fresh vegetables. This version, made with part skim-milk mozzarella and a skim-milk béchamel, captures the flavor, but not the fat of the original recipe.

1 medium-size eggplant (about 1½ pounds), stem end discarded and cut into 1-inch cubes
Kosher salt, optional
1 tablespoon olive oil
1 large clove garlic, pressed or finely minced
1 small onion, chopped (to yield about ¾ cup)
1 small carrot, finely chopped (to yield about ½ cup)
1 rib celery, finely chopped (to yield about ½ cup)
1 cup 1-inch pieces string beans
½ medium yellow bell pepper, stemmed, seeded, and diced (to yield about ½ cup)

3 cups chopped canned tomatoes with their juice
1 teaspoon vegetable oil
2 tablespoons finely chopped red onion or shallots
3 tablespoons unbleached flour
2 cups hot skim milk
About ½ pound dry lasagna noodles, enough to make 3 layers
1 pound skim-milk mozzarella cheese, coarsely grated

Place the cubed eggplant in a large colander. Sprinkle liberally with salt and allow to stand and drain 30 minutes.

Heat the oil in a large saucepan over medium-high heat. Add the garlic, onion, carrot, and celery. Cook, stirring, until the onion begins to soften, 2 to 3 minutes. Add the eggplant, string beans, and yellow pepper. Continue cooking 2 to 3 minutes longer. Add the tomatoes; season with salt, if desired. Lower the heat to medium-low; cook, stirring occasionally, until the vegetables are tender, about 30 minutes longer.

Prepare the béchamel sauce. Heat the vegetable oil in a small saucepan over medium heat. Add the red onion. Cook, stirring, until the onion begins to soften, 2 to 3 minutes. Stir in the flour and a teaspoon of salt. Cook, stirring, 1 to 2 minutes longer. The mixture will be very dry. Turn off the heat. Add the hot milk gradually to the flour-and-onion mixture while stirring briskly with a wire whisk. When all the milk is added, turn the heat to medium and continue to cook until the milk thickens and is the consistency of heavy cream, 5 to 7 minutes. Turn off the heat; set aside.

Meanwhile, bring a large pot of water to a rolling boil over high heat. Add the lasagna noodles. Cook, stirring occasionally, until the pasta is tender but firm, *al dente*, 7 to 10 minutes. Drain; rinse and separate the noodles so they don't stick together.

Preheat the oven to 350°F. Assemble the lasagna in a

9 × 13 × 3-inch glass, ceramic, or enamel-coated baking dish. Spoon 2 to 3 tablespoons of the vegetable sauce over the bottom of the pan. Arrange 3 noodles side by side in the bottom of the pan. The noodles can overlap, but they shouldn't come up the sides of the dish. If they are too long, trim them with a small sharp knife or kitchen shears. Spread 1½ to 2 cups of the vegetable sauce over the noodles. Pour ½ cup of the béchamel sauce over the vegetable sauce; spread with a spatula to distribute it evenly. Top with a third of the grated mozzarella. Repeat, adding another layer of lasagna noodles, vegetable sauce, béchamel sauce, and cheese. Top with a layer of lasagna noodles, béchamel sauce, and cheese. Cover the baking dish securely with aluminum foil. Place in the oven, on the middle rack. Bake 45 minutes. Remove the foil and bake until the top is lightly browned and bubbly, about 15 minutes longer. Allow to stand 10 minutes before serving.

ANGEL HAIR AND EGG WHITE FRITTATA WITH BROCCOLI AND MUSHROOMS

1 TO 2 SERVINGS

I learned about egg white omelets at the Canyon Ranch health spa in Tucson, Arizona. Now they're popular even at the Kosher deli near my home. This version includes some angel hair pasta, and it makes a delicious and satisfying luncheon main course with almost no fat. This recipe makes one generous serving or two modest servings.

1 teaspoon olive oil (or use oil spray)
½ cup finely chopped broccoli florets (stem and tops should be chopped)
½ cup finely sliced white mushrooms
¼ cup plus 1 tablespoon water
½ cup cooked angel hair pasta (about 1 ounce)
3 egg whites
Kosher salt, optional
Freshly ground black pepper

Wipe or spray the surface of a 10-inch nonstick skillet with oil and place over medium-high heat. When the pan is hot, add the broccoli, mushrooms, and water. Cook 5 to 7 minutes until the water has completely evaporated, the broccoli is tender, and the mushrooms are beginning to brown. Add the pasta; cook 1 minute longer. Distribute the pasta and vegetable mixture as evenly as possible over the bottom of the pan.

Beat the egg whites with the tablespoon of water; slowly pour over the pasta and vegetables. Try to cover as much surface of the pan with the egg whites as possible, lifting and tilting the pan to distribute the egg whites evenly over the bottom of the pan. Season with salt and pepper to taste, if desired. Allow to cook 5 to 7 minutes until the egg whites are firm and completely cooked through. Use a spatula to loosen the frittata from the bottom. It should hold together and move easily. Flip the frittata over in half and gently slide it from the pan onto a plate.

ORZO WITH ASPARAGUS AND HERBS

SERVES 4

Orzo is rice-shaped pasta; when cooked with broth and vegetables, it has an almost creamy consistency very much like a risotto. I recommend using a combination of different fresh herbs to give more zesty taste. This springtime dish makes the perfect accompaniment to any fish dish, or serve it as the main course for lunch with a green salad.

4 cups broth or water
1 cup dry orzo
½ pound thin asparagus spears, tough bottoms cut off and
   discarded, tips cut off and reserved, stalks coarsely chopped
2 heaping tablespoons chopped fresh herbs such as parsley,
   tarragon, chives, dill, and basil
Kosher salt, optional
Fresh ground black pepper

Bring the broth to a simmer in a medium-size saucepan over medium-high heat. Add the orzo; stir to prevent it from sticking to the bottom. Turn the heat to low; cover the pot and simmer 8 to 10 minutes until the orzo is barely tender. Remove the cover. Add the cut asparagus spears and tips. Raise the heat to medium-high; continue cooking uncovered at a steady simmer, about 5 minutes longer until the asparagus and the orzo are both tender. Some liquid should still be in the pot. Add the chopped herbs; season with salt and pepper to taste, if desired. Serve at once.

▦ NO-FAT PASTA E FAGIOLI SOUP

6 SERVINGS

The wonderful thing about pasta soups is that you can easily omit the oil without compromising the taste or texture.1 medium-size onion, finely chopped

2 small carrots, coarsely chopped
2 ribs celery, finely chopped
1 clove garlic, pressed or finely minced
$1/4$ teaspoon red pepper flakes
4 cups broth (see pages 121–26)
2 cups chopped canned tomatoes with their juice
$1/2$ cup dry tubetti, ditallini, or other small pasta
1 cup dried white kidney beans, cooked according to directions
    on pages 127–29, or one 16-ounce can cannellini beans, drained
    and rinsed well
2 tablespoons chopped fresh herbs, such as basil, parsley, thyme,
    or oregano
Kosher salt, optional
Freshly grated Parmesan cheese (optional)

In a large saucepan or 4-quart casserole combine the onion, carrots, celery, garlic, red pepper, broth, and tomatoes. Bring to a boil over medium-high heat. Reduce the heat to low; simmer, covered, until the vegetables are tender, about 15 minutes. Add the pasta; cook 10 minutes longer. Stir in the beans. Add more broth or water if the soup seems too thick. Cook until heated through, 3 to 5 minutes. Stir in the fresh herbs; season with salt to taste, if desired. Serve with Parmesan.

LOW-FAT ESCAROLE, WHITE BEAN, AND MACARONI SOUP

SERVES 6

This soup has a wonderful rich, full flavor. You can substitute greens such as Swiss chard, spinach, or even beet greens for the escarole.

1 tablespoon olive oil
2 large cloves garlic, pressed or finely minced
1 average head escarole, leaves finely chopped (to yield about
    6 cups, but exact quantity not crucial)
Kosher salt, optional
2 cups cooked white beans, either one 16-ounce can white
    cannellini beans or 1 cup dried Great Northern beans
    cooked according to the directions on pages 127–29
6 cups broth or water
1 cup dry small macaroni, tubetti, or ditallini
Freshly ground black pepper
Freshly grated Parmesan (optional)

Combine the oil and garlic in a large 4- or 6-quart saucepan or casserole over medium heat. Cook about 1 minute until the garlic begins to sizzle; add the escarole. Season with salt to taste and cook, while stirring, about 5 minutes, until the escarole is wilted and tender. Add the beans and the broth. Raise the heat to medium-high; bring the broth to a boil. Add the pasta. Cook, stirring occasionally, about 10 minutes until the pasta is tender but firm, *al dente*. Season with more salt and pepper to taste. Serve in preheated soup plates. Top with Parmesan.

SALAD OF STRING BEANS AND SUN-DRIED TOMATOES WITH A BALSAMIC, MUSTARD VINAIGRETTE

SERVES 4 TO 6

1/2 cup water
3 tablespoons balsamic vinegar
3 tablespoons red wine vinegar
1 heaping tablespoon Dijon prepared mustard
1 tablespoon extra virgin olive oil
1 teaspoon freshly ground black pepper
1 clove garlic, peeled and cut in half
1/2 pound dry penne
Kosher salt, optional
1/2 pound string beans, tips cut off and discarded
2 ounces sun-dried tomatoes (not packed in oil) cut into
    1/2-inch pieces
2 tablespoons chopped fresh parsley

In a small nonreactive mixing bowl, combine the water, balsamic and red wine vinegars, mustard, and olive oil. Mix well with a wire whisk. Stir in the black pepper and garlic. Leave at room temperature while you prepare the remaining ingredients.

Bring a large pot of water to a rolling boil over high heat. Add the penne. Cook, stirring occasionally, 7 to 10 minutes until the pasta is tender but firm, *al dente*. Drain; transfer to a large mixing bowl.

Fill a small saucepan with about 1 inch of water; bring to a boil over high heat. Place the string beans in a steaming basket; place the basket in the saucepan over the boiling water. Cover and cook 8 minutes. Drain the string beans in a colander; rinse under cold water. Add the string beans to the mixing bowl with the pasta.

Bring a small saucepan of water to a rolling boil over high heat. Add the dried tomatoes and cook 5 minutes. Drain and rinse under cold water. Add the tomatoes to the mixing bowl with the beans and pasta. Remove the garlic clove from the vinaigrette dressing and add the vinaigrette to the mixing bowl with the pasta. Toss well to combine. Stir in the parsley; season with salt to taste. Serve at room temperature.

▦ PENNE SALAD WITH CARROTS, CAULIFLOWER, AND SWEET RED PEPPER

4 SERVINGS

Cooking the vegetables in wine vinegar infuses them with lots of flavor, but be sure to rinse them well after cooking.

½ pound dry penne
Kosher salt, optional
½ cup red wine vinegar
1 cup water
1 clove garlic, peeled
1 medium carrot, cut into 2-inch matchstick strips (about 1 cup)
½ head cauliflower, cut into bite-size florets
½ medium red bell pepper, stem and seeds removed and thinly
    sliced lengthwise
1 tablespoon extra virgin olive oil
1 tablespoon fresh oregano leaves

Bring a large pot of water to boil over high heat. When the water comes to a rolling boil, add the penne. Cook, stirring occasionally, until the pasta is tender but firm, *al dente*, 7 to 10 minutes. Drain; transfer to a large mixing bowl.

Combine the wine vinegar, water, and garlic clove in a small non-aluminum saucepan over medium-high heat. Bring to a boil. Reduce the heat to low and simmer 5 minutes. Add the carrots and cauliflower. Cover and cook until the cauliflower and carrots are tender, about 5 minutes. Drain in a colander; rinse with cold water.

Taste the cauliflower. If the vinegar taste is too strong, rinse it again. Remove the garlic clove; transfer the vegetables to the pasta. Add the sliced red pepper, oil, and oregano. Cool to room temperature. Season with salt to taste, if desired.

ABOUT OREGANO

Oregano is the herb most closely associated with the cooking of southern Italy. It is widely used in the preparation of pizza, tomato sauces, and numerous vegetable antipasti. Fresh oregano has become relatively available in recent years in Italian markets and from specialty greengrocers. Dried oregano has a more intense flavor than the fresh, but as with most herbs, over time the flavor of dried oregano will weaken, so it is best to restock it annually.

Index

C

D

E

S